HACKING PARENTHOOD

HACKING PARENTHOOD

10 Mantras You Can Use Daily to Reduce the Stress of Parenting

Kimberley Moran

PUBLICATIONS

These books are available at special discounts when purchased in quantity for premiums, promotions, fundraising, and educational use. For inquiries and details, contact us at www.hacklearning.org.

Published by Times 10
Cleveland, OH
HackLearning.org

Project Management by Rebecca Morris
Cover Design by Tracey Henterly
Interior Design by Steven Plummer
Editing by Jennifer Jas
Proofreading by Nicole Francoeur

Library of Congress Control Number: 2017952618
ISBN: 978-0-9985705-7-0
First Printing: October, 2017

CONTENTS

Introduction 7
Keeping your cool in a stressful world

Mantra 1: Seek to Understand 13
Identify and respond to developmental milestones

Mantra 2: Begin at the End 25
Plan backwards no matter what it looks like now

Mantra 3: Choose to Unicycle 39
Cultivate an independent child

Mantra 4: Answer the Question Asked 49
Resist the urge to tell them everything

Mantra 5: Hungry. Angry. Lonely. Tired. (H.A.L.T.) 59
Tend to basic needs before making assumptions

Mantra 6: The Prize Is in the Process 69
Allow for thinking time

Mantra 7: Honesty Comes with Trust 81
Build relationships with children

Mantra 8: Let My Decision Stand 91
Say it once and mean it whenever possible

Mantra 9: The World Really Is Different 103
Curate what's important and block out white noise

Mantra 10: Instinct Trumps Rules 115
Trust yourself even when everyone tells you not to

Conclusion 129
Parent mantras

Parent Resource Notebook 131

Other Books in the *Hack Learning Series* 153
Hack Learning Resources 167
Meet the Author 168
Acknowledgements 170

INTRODUCTION
Keeping Your Cool in a Stressful World

THE *HACK LEARNING Series* is an education series, so what's a parenting book doing in the middle of it? As a teacher I found that a large number of the questions my students' parents asked me were actually more about parenting than teaching. These questions covered expected things like homework and studying for tests, but just as likely in any given conversation were questions like, "How come she does that at school, but not at home?" and "What can I do about his attitude when I remind him to do homework?" For nearly all of childhood, kids are in school, yet they act differently at home than at school for lots of reasons. As a result, it makes sense that the *Hack Learning Series* would also share parenting hacks. The mantras I am about to share with you can help both parents and teachers gain new ideas for staying calm and purposeful around kids, and for teaching children skills to carry into adulthood.

Hacking parenthood doesn't seem very friendly, does it? So, what does it really mean? We're given one idea about parenthood when we find out we're pregnant, or that the child we've been waiting for is ready to be adopted or fostered. We dream of an idyllic world where our children are easygoing and happy. We see ourselves in the kitchen lovingly making whole foods before the family gathers around the table in organized, peaceful perfection. But when children actually come into our lives, we are shocked to find that they are already formed human beings with character traits, likes and dislikes, strengths and weaknesses, and affinities for things like staying up all night or stuffing Ziploc bags down the toilet.

Most people will tell you, and I agree, that parenting will be the toughest job you ever have to do because it's always changing. It changes even after you've worked hard to get a handle on stuff. It changes even when you've begged it not to and told it to sit down and take a timeout. Most of these changing challenges can be brought into perspective with a few simple mantras said over and over again until you're calm and ready to follow through.

In this book, I've gathered ten short mantras aimed at cutting out the stuff that doesn't really make you a better parent, and helping you focus on what you need to do in each moment to move forward. Each mantra shows you how to assess your child within a situation, and then make a plan or use your intuition to help you and your child grow.

Mantras were created thousands of years ago by people in ancient India who understood that sound is a pathway to reaching enlightenment. Mantras became medicinal sound formulas to calm the self. Within this book, I will help you use mantras to drown out the noise of the world, a bit like sticking your fingers in your ears and shouting, "La la la la, I can't hear you!" These mantras will help you hone in on what matters most when things seem out of control. Even if you don't practice meditation, mantras can be spoken by anyone, anytime. They are simply a way to calm your mind and clear out the inner clutter so you can focus.

You'll notice that I start each Mantra (chapter) with a quote by Rumi. Maulana Jalaluddin Rumi was a 13th-century Persian poet. He is regarded as one of the greatest spiritual masters and poets of all time. He used everyday life circumstances to describe the spiritual world, and I have always loved that whenever I am considering something about my daily life, I can find something Rumi said to help me think more deeply and simply. I hope you feel the same way when you read his words.

When we decide on a mantra to guide our parenting, the simple act of repetition takes us beyond our everyday boundaries and allows our mantra to seep into who we are as parents. We create an intention behind our actions. We strengthen an extremely powerful tool—our voices. When we commit to the act of using mantras in our parenting, we are staying in touch with our deepest desires about who we want our children to be. It allows us to release, relax, and surrender to our parenting intentions.

You might even want to try it out right now. Sit with your eyes closed. Repeat this personal mantra: *I am enough.* This is your new pathway. Step out into your day or evening and embrace that mantra. Allow every parenting decision to stem from it. Watch with your own eyes how this changes your interaction and your intention behind everything that you do. You are enough. You are exactly what you need to be to help your child grow to be healthy, happy, strong, and independent.

As you dive into the book, you'll notice that we have switched up some of the typical *Hack Learning Series* chapter terminology to tie into this approach. Instead of "Hacks," we have "Mantras." Instead of "Hacks in Action," we've got "Mantras in Action." However, you'll recognize the organization from the other books in the series: The Problem, Your Mantra, What You Can Do Tomorrow, A Blueprint for Full Implementation, Overcoming Pushback, and The Mantra in Action.

In each Mantra, you'll also read about a handy tool called the Parent Resource Notebook (PRN), a journal to complement the Mantras. Like repeating a mantra consistently, writing in the PRN consistently gives you a chance to pause and reset when you feel the chaos descending. Even if you aren't a journal-writer by nature, you will never regret recording your plans and thoughts about your parenting ideas and hopes. Give it a try. It will remind you of where you've been and give you a plan for where you're headed. For those of you who are journaling newbies, we've included a PRN starter at the end of the book. It's stocked with a template for each Mantra to get you off and running with your new, valuable skill of journaling. The PRN starter also has examples of filled-in templates to give you a sense of the possibilities.

I really do use every one of these mantras to help me in my own parenting. I love them because they aren't judgmental. I get to decide what I'm going to do, but my mantras help me remain focused and consistent. I believe this is the trick to good parenting. If one of these doesn't work for you, let it go. Being flexible is also a great parenting skill. So, take the time to read about how each mantra can be used during parenthood. Try them out. I think you'll quickly find that one or two will become a regular part of your repertoire. If you aren't using all of them all the time, that's totally fine. You might not need to, but know that they are there when you need them. Keep this book handy through the earliest part of your parenthood (which lasts about nineteen years!).

SEEK TO UNDERSTAND

Identify and Respond to Developmental Milestones

Everyone has been made for some particular work, and the desire for that work has been put in every heart.
— RUMI

THE PROBLEM: CHILDREN CHANGE CONSTANTLY

YOU KNOW THOSE times when you're having a friendly conversation with your child, and suddenly, everything falls apart? You're smiling as she happily tells you about her day at school and the book she is reading, and you move to the stove to make some tea. When you return a mere ten seconds later, your child is suddenly sullen and uninterested in chatting with you. What is this? What did you do wrong? I can assure you, you've done nothing wrong.

Let's call this experience "parenting," and learn how to manage it as best we can. When we look at our children's changes, or curious lack thereof, they won't always be as easy to identify as a shift in mood. Sometimes it's a shift in competence. As in, your child seems old enough to be able to bring her own plate to the sink, but she hasn't yet demonstrated the skill or initiative, so you keep doing it for her. Sometimes it's a shift in knowledge. For example, you are planning to go to the grocery store, and watch in wonder as your child takes out a pad of paper and starts a list for you. Also, it can be a physical shift, like when you notice your child easily taking a glass down from the cupboard he could never reach before.

> **Parenting is a combination of art and science. We use the developmental milestones as our science, and our personal style as our art.**

Parenthood is a lot like sailing. You want to get from one place to another and you have a boat with a sail, but the wind keeps changing and you must tack and plan with speed in order to get where you'd like to be. Then, there's a rock in the middle of the ocean and the map doesn't even show it!

Children are constantly growing in every which way: physically, emotionally, socially, intellectually, and perhaps spiritually. Just as with sailing, it is wise to make use of a map when it exists. There are some readily available developmental charts that tell you what you can expect and when, over the course of a childhood. The weather and the course may not be exactly what the map purports; however, keeping the chart on hand as a baseline is far better than navigating without it.

Learning to look for milestones can open your eyes significantly to where your child is right now. It's easy to find loads of developmental milestone charts online; just search for "developmental milestone chart 0-19 years old." They are all pretty similar because they are based on how typical children develop. That means you might not see your child lining up, but use the ranges as background and look for milestones you do see.

As an example, take a look at milestones for five- to seven-year-olds, and you can see that expecting a child to pay attention becomes increasingly reasonable at the end of this phase. This can help you keep appropriate expectations, resulting in less-frustrating situations. You can also see that telling your five-year-old not to tattle on his siblings or friends is like asking a fish not to swim. It's a milestone that is part of being five to seven years old. Irritating for sure, but not life-threatening. Now let's consider how *Seek to Understand* works as a mantra.

YOUR MANTRA: SEEK TO UNDERSTAND

The *Seek to Understand* mantra is the cornerstone of the mantras, so I've listed it first. As a parent, you leave a lot to chance if you don't know what to expect from your child. Learning how children grow and applying that information to your child's growth will change your parenthood as you look forward to each new development. Just like you look forward to the consistent rituals around holidays and celebrations, it will be exciting when you know what to expect as your child grows. You knew your child would walk one day, and then she did!

A solid understanding of milestones and child development can benefit parents in several ways. This knowledge gives you a starting place that can be helpful in:

- Planning their environment: moving out of a crib, having bunk beds, needing a desk

- Considering their learning: reading fairy tales, learning to tell time, driving a car

- Designing learning experiences: visiting a zoo, going on a plane, sleeping away from home

- Understanding sequences: crawling, walking, understanding symbols

The more you know what to expect from your child, the more you know what to look for, which is also helpful if your child is not meeting developmental milestones. I worried when my daughter didn't want to read the books her kindergarten teacher sent home. I thought she wasn't learning as quickly as the other children. But when I researched what to expect from a five-year-old, I found that children might not understand the use of symbols (like the alphabet) until they are closer to age seven. Armed with this information, I stopped worrying. It's your job as a parent to be observant. You know your child best. Understanding where your child's development lies in the big picture helps you support your child in the best ways.

When your child does something that is different from what you've seen before, say the mantra, *Seek to Understand*, until you get to a place where you can learn more. It's not an issue until you know more about the behavior and put it into context. For example, maybe your child suddenly starts sucking his thumb. You panic because he has never indulged this habit before. You calm yourself down by repeating *Seek to Understand* because it's not going to help to yell, "Why are you doing that?!" to him. Then you check out the chart and see that your four-year-old might have lots of fears. When you connect the dots, you see that possibly this thumb-sucking is a way to soothe those fears. In this way, you can start to help him discuss his fears, and as you work through them, he will need his thumb less and less. The change in behavior becomes more understandable and easier to manage.

WHAT **YOU** CAN DO TOMORROW

- **Create a Parent Resource Notebook (PRN).** Mantras are built on repetition. All good habits are. Consider getting into the habit of using the PRN as your go-to parenting log. The PRN can be an actual notebook or a digital one. You'll want to choose a notebook you love, or if you go digital, find an app that allows easy access to your notes. I use the notes app that comes with my iPhone because I can also access it on my computer. To make things super easy, we've got a ready-made PRN at the back of this book with everything you need to get started. Get comfortable with your choice because you'll be referring and adding to it throughout your parenthood journey. In some ways this is like an app that tracks your eating or exercise. Sure, our parents didn't need this technology, but now we have complicated lives and these tools provide efficient and helpful information (see Mantra 9: The World Really Is Different!).

- **Using your PRN, write down what to expect from your child now.** Writing down where your child is developmentally takes no time at all (see Template #1). Be sure to Google a free online development chart to help you define this. Take a look at the chart based on your child's age. You might even want to print it and put it right in your PRN so you can easily refer to it.

- **Appreciate the milestones your child has already reached.** Take the time to celebrate as your children reach milestones, no matter how small. Sometimes being a parent is just about watching your child change and grow before your very eyes. In many ways it's as miraculous as watching a caterpillar become a butterfly. Here's a kid who came to you without the ability to even hold his own head up, and now he's running through the house screaming a language made of symbols and sounds, playing an instrument in the school band, or driving her own car.

- **Choose one milestone not yet reached that you want to understand.** Think deep here. What is one thing you want to understand more about your child? You can't understand everything at once, nor can you track *everything*. The more you insist on growth, the more frustrated you and your child will be. Let's say you want to understand when your child remembers to brush her teeth without a reminder. Consider the factors that led to this moment. It may seem silly, but you may also start to see what intrinsic things motivate a particular child.

A BLUEPRINT FOR FULL IMPLEMENTATION

Step 1: Arm yourself (and anyone else caring for your child) with information.

Conduct a Google search for "developmental milestones 0-19 years old." Several reputable results will turn up. Pick one and study the chart. What rings true to you about your child, and what parts should you leave on the cutting floor (so to speak)? Milestones were created to help provide a bit of a map, but they are not intended to make you feel badly about where your child is. Childhood is an incomplete science. We must use information that makes sense and discard the rest.

This doesn't mean that you shouldn't wonder (even out loud to your pediatrician) why your child isn't meeting milestones or is skipping some. It never hurts to share. In fact, you'll want everyone who regularly interacts with your child to understand your child's development. Yes, even teachers. They spend so much time with your child and may have seen milestone behavior that you thought your child hadn't yet reached. I've seen my son's teachers look both surprised and pleased when I tell them about milestones I've observed at home. Teachers don't need to do anything extra for your child, but it can help them to know that you are focusing on understanding your child's growth toward independence in all areas.

Step 2: Make your PRN a habit.

Don't assume you're going to remember all this developmental information. It's hard enough dealing with the young person right in front of you, and when you add milestones met and milestones yet to meet, it can be easy to feel overwhelmed. Don't. Write in your PRN and then you'll know it will be there when you need it. I've pulled out my PRN notes on my iPhone in the middle of dinner to show my husband what we're seeing. Knowledge is power, and in this case, knowledge can lower our blood pressure and remind us that it takes time for kids to grow and mature. Use your PRN as the key to accessing as much of your power as possible. Committing to your PRN is trusting yourself and your process. You can do this.

Step 3: Go slowly and stay flexible.

When people start something new, they often want to know what to expect, and they want to be good at it right away. Unfortunately, parenthood isn't an exact science. Parenting is a combination of art and science. We use the developmental milestones as our science, and our personal style as our art. I might want to see my kids back up their opinions with facts, but what I see is bickering and talking back. I have to remind myself that this behavior is appropriate for kids eleven to thirteen years old. It says right on the chart that kids this age need opportunities to make decisions. It also says that even if the child is negative or rebellious, it is important for parents to focus on developing the child's self-value. I have to be flexible in my expectation of what I see and how I react.

How can you tweak what's happening in the moment using your understanding? Do you need to simplify your expectations? Did you plan for a thirteen-year-old's reaction when your child is only ten? It's easy to do this. Just rethink it and set a more achievable goal.

What do you think your child can do successfully right now? Slow down and *Seek to Understand*. This will take conscious mental effort and self-reminding at first. Keep at it. It will become second nature soon enough.

OVERCOMING PUSHBACK

You might encounter pushback from family, friends, and nosy acquaintances, especially as you integrate the PRN in your quest to *Seek to Understand*. You might even push back against the idea yourself. After all, integrating new habits and new mindsets takes time. Remind yourself and others that parenting is hard at some point nearly every day, especially when we are unclear about the milestones. That's why pregnant and new parents arm themselves with information in order to better understand the process they are witnessing firsthand.

Why do you need a notebook? In my day... Whether you have a partner in this parenting business or just someone who occasionally spends time with you and your child, it may be necessary to explain your PRN. Your response may be as simple as stating that your PRN is a little like a baby book or a scrapbook. It's designed to remind you of things you don't want to forget and to record your memories.

I don't have time to write everything down. This is where you need to give yourself a good talking to. There is proof that writing down important ideas and goals helps bring them to fruition. In the case of the PRN, it does several things. First, it brings you (and anyone who you do this with) to a quiet space for focused thinking about parenting. Second, writing ideas down helps you refine them and make them yours. Third, writing down milestones helps shed light on your child's growth. Sure, things will be accomplished without writing them down, but not as intentionally, and you won't know when you've reached a milestone and can move on.

Following someone else's rules is so much easier. It's true! This may be the toughest pushback because parenting books everywhere tell you exactly what to do, when, and why. If experts have already laid out the milestones, why do you need to reflect on them? The books are simply tools, and in the end, no one knows you, your partner, your child, or your environment better than you do. You are the best person to understand your child's development, and your PRN can guide you.

THE MANTRA IN ACTION

When my children were five and seven, they suddenly moved from being shy, quiet kids to extremely loud beings. When I checked out a developmental chart for what to expect from a child ages five to seven, I read: Five- to seven-year-olds may be prone to people pleasing, more regulated acceptable emotions, bragging and boasting about accomplishments, interested in the rules, acting silly when tired, having lots of fears, having a temper, and *being quite noisy.*

That's a LOT of good information. I actually laughed as I read it. It was so close to what I was seeing. It also gave me permission to accept that my children are supposed to be noisy at this time in their lives. This didn't seem like a good time to expect them to listen quietly, did it? Yet, that's just what I had begun to do because I was so sick of them being so darn loud all of a sudden! So I switched gears. If they were going to be noisemakers for a few years, I could at least try to focus that energy on activities that would be good for their physical and intellectual health. I could make sure they get to run around outside and be as loud as they want.

I also got them into a singing program and started asking them to talk about things more often. They wanted to talk. It came easy to them. This was when we began to talk about the difference between discussion and argument. This was also when we set rules about ditching electronics during outside playtime. I explained to them exactly what I was thinking and why I, the parent, was pushing them out the door to play without the distraction of electronics. It was hard to argue with my logic. I mean, they did argue because they had a close personal relationship with their electronics, but they saw my point.

Celebrate the phase your children are in instead of shutting it down. Also, be kind to the insecurities that come with different phases and take the associated fears seriously. Ages five to seven may be a good time to teach and model self-soothing techniques at bedtime. Remember, they may have very real fears about being alone in the dark. Instead of discounting these fears, meet them head on and make intentional decisions together about how your child will handle scary situations. Your knowledge gained about milestones will be important when you consider what you want for your child when he or she is grown.

Once you understand what you are seeing, it is easier to construct rules that make sense for this point in time in this particular child's life. This *Seek to Understand* mantra starts by acknowledging that children change constantly. Keep that in mind. Whatever annoying behavior or trait you are seeing will probably pass pretty soon. If children learn to be okay with where they are and focus on what they can change, they will be more flexible, confident adults. *Seek to Understand* grounds everything else you do as a parent.

Allow yourself to experience the wonder in each phase of your child's development, and recognize that *Seek to Understand* is enough for today. It may help you make it through one day without feeling like you need to do more than simply understand.

MANTRA 2

BEGIN AT THE END

Plan Backwards No Matter What It Looks Like Now

You were born with wings. You are not meant for crawling, so don't.
— RUMI

THE PROBLEM: SETTING BOUNDARIES CAUSES FEAR AND GUILT

WHEN A NEW, beautiful, tiny person comes to live in your house for the first time, the last thing you're thinking about is setting boundaries. You are simply basking in the literal miracle of having a new, beautiful, tiny person. After about one hour of bliss—if you're that lucky—people will start telling you how you need to have rules for sleeping, eating, talking, crawling, and yes, even breathing. It seems that nothing can be accomplished in parenting without outsiders suggesting rules.

A boundary is just another way of saying "a step on the path to successfully reaching a milestone." For example, if you want your child to monitor her use of electronics on her own, you have to set a boundary for what is acceptable use. How else will she practice the skill that leads to the milestone? Creating boundaries is a fact of raising children, but knowing what those limits should be—what each incremental step will be—is open to interpretation. Parents feel fear and guilt over many of the lines they draw, especially when others issue judgment so readily. It would be lovely if all we had to do as parents is get up each day and admire our small people, but it isn't reality.

If you're like most parents, you've spent many hours agonizing over every aspect of your child's life. You know you want your child to be safe and happy, but you also want her to be independent, organized, successful, kind, appropriately competitive, honest, and brave. There's so much that you want, in fact, that these feelings of fear and guilt may stop you from setting the boundaries needed to create a sane, safe, and stimulating family life. Take a minute to consider which boundaries are the most important to you right now.

Here are some examples of what you might want your child to do:

- Sleep in his/her own bed
- Turn off electronics by a certain time
- Eat mostly healthy food
- Apologize when being unkind
- Read every day
- Play sports

In a typical day of parenting, ideas for boundaries can come up nearly every other hour. You'll want to be prepared to make decisions that work best for your family. Since we're all very different people and our children are equally different, it's important to recognize that you might make different choices or define different boundaries than anyone else you know. This is not only okay; it's awesome.

Differences are inevitable, but they should not stop you from using parenting ideas to develop your boundaries. There are so many out there that you'll need a system for identifying which parenting ideas will help you get your child where you want him/her to be. Imagine how peaceful it could be if you had a way to think about the boundaries you set, and move forward with confidence.

YOUR MANTRA: BEGIN AT THE END

By identifying what you want for your child in the long term, you'll be able to set more clearly defined boundaries for each short-term situation. One of the best ways to understand how this works is by considering a St. Bernard puppy.

St. Bernard dogs are beautiful. They are fluffy and have big square heads that demand to be petted. As puppies, they are big enough to wrestle with but small enough to pull right into your lap. It's delightful how their paws smell like Fritos and so you can't resist letting them put both paws on your shoulders. It's also irresistible when they rest their head in your lap during dinner while you feed them small pieces of steak. They're babies, for heaven's sake, you think to yourself. The problem is that when that fluffy baby grows up, a St. Bernard can be thirty-five inches tall and up to two hundred and sixty pounds. Then, it's not so cute or practical to have them under the table or crushing your lap.

With the *Begin at the End* plan, you don't let that cute puppy on your lap, on the couch, or under your table, because you don't want to condition it to keep those behaviors into adulthood. Instead, you get down on the floor to do your petting and paw-smelling, because you know this is something you will always be able to do. Now it will be true that some people are fine with their couches getting ruined by their dogs, or that the kitchen table moves up and down with the dog under it. It's your own vision of the end that matters, not anyone else's. They don't have to set that boundary, but you do if you want to end up with a clean couch and a peaceful dinnertime.

> When you *Begin at the End*, you remember to play the long game, which ends with an independent, responsible adult.

There won't be a need for re-training when you plan backwards. That said, you must identify what your end looks like. You must make conscious choices and decisions about what kinds of experiences you want for yourself and your child before you can set shorter-term boundaries. Note: Don't panic about how long it may take to reach the end. You are in this for the long haul, right? You are merely keeping the end in sight one day at a time.

WHAT **YOU** CAN DO TOMORROW

Making decisions about what you want your children to be like when they grow up can feel overwhelming, but not when you start small.

- **Choose one milestone and set up a plan, remembering to *Begin at the End*.** What is the one milestone you'd like to focus on and what rules must be in place to make sure your child has the best chance of long-term success in meeting an end goal? For example, one end goal might be, "My child will become someone who is organized and can manage her belongings." When we *Begin at the End,* we can see the steps to that end more clearly. One way to help your child learn to do this is to expect her to clean her own room. Write this end goal and first step in your PRN so that you will remember it later.

- **Try it.** If this goal is the one you are working on, make sure to show your child what her room looks like when it's clean. It should be obvious where things go so that she doesn't need to come to you to ask how to do something. You might want to wait until her room is messy but not overwhelming. Ask her what

> she thinks she should do step-by-step to clean the room. Then, let her at it.
>
> - **Reflect.** Read what you wrote in your PRN about this one step in relation to the end goal. Give yourself ten minutes to write about how it felt to *Begin at the End.*

A BLUEPRINT FOR FULL IMPLEMENTATION

Step 1: Develop boundaries and corresponding small steps.

Identify a list of traits and behaviors (also called milestones) you hope your child will develop. If you are having trouble developing the list, find a tribe of parents on Facebook or Twitter who can offer up ideas. Use the following list of traits common among responsible adults to trigger your thoughts:

- Manage personal finances
- Think for oneself
- Read to entertain or inform
- Follow through on a passion
- Find motivation for an activity
- Have a conversation
- Feel compassion for others
- Listen appropriately
- Drive and care for a car
- Clean a room
- Put oneself to sleep
- Make a meal or snack

- Organize things
- Be present in a moment

Next, work out a list of three to five steps or boundaries to reach the trait you most want your child to learn. Remember the mantra, *Begin at the End*, with every boundary you define. This is really where the rubber meets the road because if you aren't clear in your own mind, then your children will learn to bypass the system. They are tricky that way, aren't they? You might need to compromise to make things work. Use your PRN to write down everything you've talked about and decided (see Template #2). Put the date on your pages so you'll know how long it's been since you considered these steps.

Step 2: Find an in-person or online support group.

As with any endeavor related to children, asking for support or advice can be quite helpful when executing a long-term plan. While it might be possible to set boundaries and stick to them without any help from anyone else, it is less likely. Even the most confident person in the world can buckle as a parent during a major tantrum involving a two-year-old or a thirteen-year-old. During a time like this, it'll be important to fall back on your mantra, *Begin at the End*, so you can think about how to react to your child's loss of control. Check out Twitter, Facebook, or a local neighborhood parenting group to find like-minded individuals who will support you when those around you might not. Knowing you have someone who can empathize with your situation and knows how much this means to you can be reassuring and can make trusting yourself easier. In addition, it is proven in businesses and nonprofits all over that having an accessible hive of supporters and information-gatherers increases success.

Step 3: Be consistent and clear.

Do not assume anything about what your child understands or can do. It is important to provide models for what each step looks like. No matter how young or old your child is, explain why you've decided on this boundary and what it means.

- *Younger child example*: I want you to brush your teeth twice a day because teeth affect your health. If your teeth are dirty or have cavities, it can make your body feel sick.

- *Older child example*: I need to make sure you are safe and well. So, you need to be at the dinner table with the whole family three times a week. This gives me time to check in with you and make sure you are eating well.

Set boundaries that can stay put for a while. For example, if your schedule is such that your child cannot be home every single day at 4 p.m. to start homework, then, of course, you won't want to set a rule that he must start homework by 4 p.m. Instead, you could consider making a rule that your child must check in to assess and complete homework daily before 7 p.m. Consistency will help you *Begin at the End*.

Step 4: Establish check-in times for adults.

Pull out your PRN any time you want to reflect on your plan or how its daily operations are going. Some people might want to write in it every Sunday. Establish a check-in time at least once a month. It might be a good idea to check in with an online support group or a partner, family member, or friend. Discuss what's going well and what could be tweaked. Congratulate yourself on being a thoughtful, responsible parent who cares enough to right the ship regularly, even if you might do things wrong every day just like every other parent. During these quick check-ins, be sure to consider if your child is ready for a new step closer to the end goal.

Step 5: Revisit boundaries with your child.

Just because you tell your child what you'd like to see from her, doesn't mean she is suddenly going to do it happily and regularly. We aren't miracle workers, just hackers! She may need quite a bit of monitoring as she develops in the chosen skill areas, but at least now you'll have a rationale to share with your child to bolster you when you feel like throwing in the towel. It will help your child to see that the boundaries you've chosen have a purpose. You are choosing to *Begin at the End* every time you connect a boundary to an end goal.

OVERCOMING PUSHBACK

Parenting is a sensitive endeavor, so your decision to choose what matters to you most in the end and setting boundaries around your end goals may affect people in peculiar ways. Here are some possible negative reactions by others or yourself, and my suggestions for responding:

Some people will say, "Your boundaries will fail." There are always going to be people who disagree with the way you parent because of the many factors that are involved in parenting decision-making. The truth is that sometimes you will fail, so they are right. This system is not designed to stop failure; it can only help you manage your boundaries in a flexible manner. You can safely say to these naysayers, "I know. That's how I learn what works and what doesn't." No one can argue with someone who agrees with them.

Parenting shouldn't be so prescribed. What's so great about the mantra *Begin at the End* is that you can feel good about how you choose to go off the intended path. You've done your work, so you know what steps or boundaries are important for you to teach as your child's parent, but you also know that a bit of flexibility can be helpful. A homework routine might be an important lesson toward the end goal of being responsible for one's own learning, but there may be a time when family trumps homework. Starr Sackstein and Connie Hamilton provide many strategies for inspiring learning at home in *Hacking Homework*. It is those occasions when you will explain to your child why the choice has been made so that she can learn to prioritize later in life.

The future is unpredictable. How can I possibly have an end in mind when so much changes so quickly? Considering end goals can feel overwhelming. It's important to focus on what you think makes a responsible adult. There are lots of ways to get ideas for this, ranging from a simple Google search to asking people at dinner parties. Some will resonate with you and some will fall flat. Keep your PRN with you so you can write down great ideas when you hear them. That's why I use the notes feature on my iPhone as my PRN. I always have my phone with me and it's easy to use voice dictation to get the thought down.

I have trouble sticking to boundaries. If this is you, you're in good company. The majority of parents have great intentions, but lack follow-through. Life gets busy and we tend to be more willing to let things go most days. But when you take the mantra *Begin at the End* to heart, your rationale will change. Now you aren't just asking a child to clean his room because you like a clean house; instead you want your child to become a responsible, organized adult. Keep this in mind when you feel yourself losing resolve to stick to the boundaries. What do you want in the long run?

THE MANTRA IN ACTION

Parenting is a tough and sometimes lonely challenge. In writing this book, I found myself revisiting my previously set boundaries and wondering if it was time to update them. Recently homework has become a particularly turbulent activity in our house. It used to be simple to get my children to sit down and work on a sheet of math problems or read two chapters of a book, but as my children get older it's clear that the homework reflects something they've learned during the day. This means that I can't always be as helpful as I used to be. After all, I'm not in their classes. My kids also seem so tired and this makes me, quite frankly, a little angry about the homework.

My end goal for my children is that they will be able to listen to an assignment, write it down, ask questions to clarify it, make time to do the work, and accomplish it by the due date. This is a skill they must use for the rest of their lives. For a long time, I would ask them what they had to do for homework and then I would make sure they sat down to do it before dinner and bed-time. As my children are now in upper elementary and middle grades, I think they need to be able to do this on their own. That said, I know there will be some failure involved, but the challenges are worth it because we have a valuable end in mind.

My husband and I sit down together to revisit our homework rules. We record our new rules in the PRN. We marvel at how great we are, really, because this part of parenting is hard. Then, we tell our kids what we expect them to do on their own:

1. Your work must be completed before 8 p.m.

2. You may not hand in work late to a teacher.

3. You must be willing to ask questions when you don't understand.

4. We are on hand to coach you through an assignment or on writing questions about an assignment, but we won't keep you on task or ask your teacher questions for you.

That said, we stay out of their way. Recently I was delighted to see that my typically disorganized son got all As and Bs without needing me to remind him of anything. However, he made a unilateral and silent decision not to do an online part of his homework which is why he got a B- in Spanish. So, I reminded him that our rules state that you may not hand in work late. Despite his protests that he was fine with a B-, he agreed that he did not follow the rule and would do so next time.

There was a fight about it to be sure, but we won because we could explain how important it was to us that he is someone who can be trusted with an assignment. We showed him the thought that we put into it. We were consistent. We didn't feel bad because we kept our end goal in sight.

You might be asking yourself, "What's the consequence?" As in, do your kids ever get punished? I believe in natural consequences for the most part because I am trying to teach a young person what an older person must learn. When consequences are not self-evident to children, they should be written in the rules, and they should be relevant to the rules. Making a consequence arbitrary is not a learning experience. For example, after rule number two above, you might write: If work is handed in late, you lose electronics for each day the homework was late. The best way to look at a consequence is, "What part of the boundary was disrespected?" If it was in not listening, then give them a consequence that involves more listening practice. If it was in not doing a chore, give them more time to practice that chore. The above example of removing electronics gives them more time to accomplish the homework they weren't doing.

When we try things with our kids and they don't work, it can be tempting to throw the baby out with the bathwater. The mantra *Begin at the End* will help you remember that if one thing doesn't work, another boundary might. If your child is having trouble accomplishing the step you've developed, maybe it's time to dial it back even more. Trust the process by thinking about a step before where your child is now. It's a slow process on some days and a super-fast connection on others. When you *Begin at the End*, you remember to play the long game, which ends with an independent, responsible adult.

MANTRA 3

CHOOSE TO UNICYCLE

Cultivate an Independent Child

It's your road, and yours alone. Others may walk it with you, but no one can walk it for you.
— Rumi

THE PROBLEM: CHILDREN AREN'T DOING MUCH ON THEIR OWN

CHILDREN NEED ADULTS to help them with things. The parenting question lies in when they can start doing things for themselves. We all laugh at the parent who holds his son's toast between bites or spoon-feeds a six-year-old while the kid is watching a screen. "I just want him to eat," the parent will sheepishly explain. There is a difference between a child needing an adult to do things and an adult not letting a child do things. My child cannot reach the plates in the cupboard. They are too high. I can give her a stool, move the plates to a lower cupboard, or hand her the plates until she is over five feet tall. In this example, we start to see the point, but the problem goes much deeper.

It is universally known that a child's independence is bittersweet. It happens quickly if you let it. Does the speed of independence depend on you, the parent—or the skill set of your child? It's a bit of both.

THE MANTRA: CHOOSE TO UNICYCLE

The unicycle is a universal symbol both for the number one and for the ability to balance. To learn more about how independent my kids are, I created the Unicycle Chart. When you and your family fill in this chart, you're going to know exactly what independent skills your child is working on right now. The chart can be as simple as a small whiteboard, sectioned off with Washi tape or permanent marker. We've also included a sample called Template #3 as an option. Keep the chart in the kitchen or another well-trafficked area in your home where you'll all see it regularly and remember to use it. You'll still have your PRN for planning, but the chart is a helpful visual for tracking. Every time you look at that chart, it will jog your memory to *Choose to Unicycle* when it comes to your kids. This is where you might ask yourself: "What are ways to let him be more independent? What can I stop doing so she can do it on her own?"

It's always good to see the truth in black and white. There

> This chart system is specific and measurable, which shows your child how to develop, track, and achieve goals.

are so many times we say things like, "He is up every night," because it feels like that when you're tired, but now you're going to use this board to see the truth. It couldn't be any easier. You'll only have two categories: the things you want to see (Skills) and how many times you see them (Tallies). See Template #3 for an example and a template you can use right now for your own Unicycle Chart.

When members of your family see this chart, they will know what to look for. They can positively reinforce the child in factual ways: "Hey! You found your stuff four times this week! Awesome." When it seems like your child has chosen to unicycle this skill, say after a month of doing it nearly every day, you can change to a new skill. Remember to remind your child that the mastered skill is now an expectation.

This chart system is specific and measurable, which shows your child how to develop, track, and achieve goals. It is also a great way to positively reinforce your child in meaningful ways. No more, "You are a good boy or girl," which means nothing. Now you have a concrete skill to compliment or discuss in a realistic way. The second benefit to the Unicycle Chart is that you (the parent) are reinforced as well. Not only have you recognized that independence has value, but you've done something about it. When your child drops the cup she is bringing to the sink (by herself!), slow down and say your mantra, *Choose to Unicycle*, to remind yourself that you are intentionally parenting, and she is learning independence.

WHAT **YOU** CAN DO TOMORROW

Remembering to use the Unicycle Chart will take some practice, but you'll be surprised how your children will remind you it's there.

- **Post your Unicycle Chart.** Choose the material for your chart—a whiteboard, chalkboard, or Template #3—and tape it up in the kitchen where everyone will see it.

- **Use your PRN to choose one independent skill.** It should be something clear and trackable: set the table, put clothes in the hamper, pack backpack for tomorrow.

- **Tell the kids what you're tracking, how, and why.** It is important for them to understand the goal. "I want you to be able to make your bed by yourself, so every time you do, I'll put a tally mark on the Unicycle Chart. My goal for you is five times a week."

- **Start tracking.** Tally up the times that skill is accomplished completely independently. That means WITHOUT reminding. This is the key to knowing when someone is truly choosing to unicycle—when she can do it independently without reminders and while doing other things in her life as well.

A BLUEPRINT FOR FULL IMPLEMENTATION

Step 1: Have a family meeting.

Explain to your family that a huge part of being a parent lies in teaching a child how to *Choose to Unicycle*. This is what you'll call going it alone and maintaining balance—doing things independently. Tell them that this job is one that you take seriously. The reward is a child who can manage life on his/her own. You want this for your child. Independence is a part of growing up. Discuss the idea of how a unicycle symbolizes one and balance. At this point, everyone may stop paying attention to you and ask for a unicycle. They may even discuss who would be a better unicyclist. After letting this go on for a moment, call them back to order and let them know that they can become (metaphorical) unicyclists at home.

Step 2: Personalize the Unicycle Chart.

Decide on your final iteration of the Unicycle Chart. Whether it's a whiteboard, piece of paper, or an app on your phone, there will still be two columns: Skills and Tallies. For each child in your house, share five skills you'd like them to begin working on, but ask them to choose just two or three. Make sure those skills are achievable and developmentally appropriate. Use a different color for each child. Let them write or type their new skill goals on the chart.

Step 3: Practice the skill with each child.

Don't make the skill more difficult than it needs to be. If you want your child to make his bed, put one comforter and a pillow on it. Sheets, blankets, and a bedspread can come later—maybe even after he gets out of college! Keep expectations appropriate and possible. Say cheerfully, "Here's how you can do this on your own," then model it. Next, ask him to do the same thing. "You give it a try. See! You can do it."

Step 4: Set a tally goal and a time frame.

Give your child time to turn the skill into an independent routine. Set explicit rules around accomplishing this goal. Does she have to do it within a twenty-four-hour period or a two-hour period? Does a successfully achieved goal mean he gets a tally five to seven times a week for two weeks? If so, use the first week to set a goal of two to three times a week without reminders, but make sure he completes that skill seven days a week, regardless. He doesn't get out of it just because he needed a reminder, but he doesn't get a tally for that day.

Step 5: Don't remind him too soon.

If you want someone to do something independently, you have to allow for personality and daily fluctuations. There are lots of times you might make your bed right when you wake up, but sometimes it happens later in the day. If he wants to make his bed before breakfast, that's great, but if he rushes upstairs to do it before he leaves for school that's equally wonderful. Don't remind him until he returns from school and the bed still isn't made. Then, have him make it to build muscle memory and don't give him a tally.

Step 6: Incentivize it.

Once a goal is achieved regularly and you are ready to work on a new skill, give children incentives for completion. Every family is different. You might add twenty-five cents to an allowance. You might give the child an experience that he has been waiting to be old enough to do. You decide. These are great ways to help kids see that becoming independent is hard work but has benefits.

OVERCOMING PUSHBACK

Making Unicycle Charts work well requires participation and consistency. You'll need to be ready to respond to pushback from yourself or others.

There are so many things to work on, are we going to track all of them? Many skills make up a complete person, true enough, but you're only going to choose two or three that your child will work on regularly. After a while these skills will become seamless and it will make sense to drop them from the chart. Then you can shift attention to new ones. If using a Unicycle Chart made of paper, consider keeping successfully completed charts in a folder. Take them out on New Year's Day, a birthday, or the end of the school year to celebrate your child's growing skill set. If using a whiteboard or chalkboard, you could accomplish this by taking and saving pictures.

I can't carry a chart with me everywhere I go. While this is a valid point, there are options. You could take a picture of the chart on your phone and add tally marks to the image while you are away from home, such as for the skill, "Responsible for own belongings." Or, you could add the tallies to your chart when you get home. Note that your child may achieve a skill when you're not around to observe, like when he's in school or at a friend's house. You won't be able to track everything your child does, nor should you. Keep it simple by tracking the skills you see at home, which is under your control and where you spend a lot of your time.

I can't spend my time tracking behaviors. Of course you can. You already do. Only right now you're either doing it yourself when it isn't complete or you're getting angry at your child. Neither action is helping your child *Choose to Unicycle*. It's actually a simple, fun way to see what your child can do now and in the future. It will be exciting to watch your children succeed by using the Unicycle Chart. It will also help them build their own intrinsic motivation for choosing to unicycle. The more concrete you make development and reaching milestones, the more likely your child will be proud to accomplish them. Remember how exciting it was for them to sit up, crawl, walk, and feed themselves?

THE MANTRA IN ACTION

Katelynn Spear is the mother of a seven-year-old daughter, Olivia. Katelynn has fifteen years of experience working with toddlers and elementary-aged children at her mother's childcare center in Freeport, Maine, so using a chart felt like second nature to Katelynn when Olivia started going to preschool. And now that Olivia is in second grade, using her Unicycle Chart is just a regular part of her day.

"One way to get started is to be sure the chores on your chart are easily understood by your kids and that the chores are tailored to their age levels and your household expectations," said Katelynn. "Children as young as two can carry out simple chores like collecting the bathroom garbage cans or helping to pick up toys. Teenagers might be much more involved helpers, perhaps doing yard work, laundry, and other household chores that will prepare them for life on their own."

"Olivia chooses one chore each week that she wants to do or help with, and moves it from the pink strip over to the corner of the chore chart. It sticks using Velcro. I'll admit that sometimes during the week she may not want to help with the thing she's chosen, but I'm flexible about letting her pick a different thing to do. It's more to get her into the routine of helping out and learning how to do things on her own."

Here are some of the chores Katelynn has asked Olivia to do:

- Clear and set the table
- Dust
- Help cook and prepare food
- Carry and put away groceries
- Take care of pets
- Vacuum and mop
- Take out the trash
- Fold and put away laundry

"These are all things my mother asked of me around this age, and I want Olivia to be able to do them on her own. Also, Olivia seems so happy when she accomplishes things. She might be mad going into the activity when she'd rather be doing something else, but she is visibly happier when she has completed a job well done."

Encouraging children to embrace personal independence is a critical parenting goal. With it comes confidence, less reliance on others, less stress, better decision-making skills, increased self-esteem, and broader horizons. *Choose to Unicycle* is a simple way to make big things happen for your child, and to celebrate the successes together.

ANSWER THE QUESTION ASKED

Resist the Urge to Tell Them Everything

Look for the answer inside your question.
— RUMI

THE PROBLEM: PARENTS OVERCOMPLICATE PARENTING

IT'S A NEW and wonderful thing that parents and children are communicating more than ever. Many subjects that once were taboo are being talked about in ways never before discussed. So, when is talking about something not a great idea? The short answer: When your child is getting more information than she can process. Often children ask questions and we answer them in an overcomplicated way. For example:

Simple

Asked: "Are you going to die?"

Answer: "Yes, all living things die, but I've got lots of time to spend with you."

Overcomplicated

Asked: "Are you going to die?"

Answer: "Yes, all living things die. Some people believe that people go to heaven. Heaven is a place in the sky where everything is happy. Some people believe that we become other things. This is called reincarnation. Some people believe nothing happens after we die, but that all matter just changes shape."

Get it? This is an exaggerated example, of course, but even this conversation happens. Parents tend to overcomplicate conversations because they've been thinking about a topic for a long time and once a question remotely resembling it comes up, the floodgates of information open. Stick to the question asked as much as possible so that your child can process the information properly. He may eventually want to know what you think happens after you die, and this will be when you choose to explain what you believe and what you know others to believe.

THE MANTRA: ANSWER THE QUESTION ASKED

When parents hear me say that one of the mantras is to *Answer the Question Asked*, they usually laugh. We've all been there, and we all seem to keep going there. Parenting would be much easier if we would stop overcomplicating things. In fact, *Answer the Question Asked* may also help you and your partner agree more often about the way information is delivered to a child, instead of saying, "I wouldn't have said it like that!" With this mantra,

> The simpler we are in our answers and reactions, the more likely children are to trust us enough to be honest with us. Learning to *Answer the Question Asked* is transformative for both child and parent.

the expectation is that you will respect your child's natural curiosity without giving him too much to handle.

One great way to stop yourself from going on and on is to turn part of the question back onto your child. If the question is, "Why do we have to go visit Grandma every week?" explain briefly that you like to check in to make sure she's safe and then ask this question back, "Why do people visit each other?" The more your child gets accustomed to thinking about questions and not having you fill in all the blanks, the better he will become at questioning.

Asking good questions is a centerpiece of learning and living. It's a skill we use every day, on everything from choosing our lunch to searching for the right products at Target. So much of our success in life depends on asking the right questions. If we over-complicate the answers to our kids' questions, we push them away from wanting to ask the questions. Plan to *Answer the Question Asked* to help you keep things simple.

WHAT **YOU** CAN DO TOMORROW

These ideas can be started tomorrow, and you may end up practicing them for the entirety of your parenting experience. They are well worth the thought and time.

- **Start small.** Remember that, "Are you going to die?" example in the beginning of this chapter? Try answering everything as simply as possible no matter what the topic. When your child asks you questions like, "What are we having for dinner?" Think of the simplest way to answer it and say that, such as, "macaroni and cheese." When your child asks you why he has to wear his boots, you can answer, "Because they protect your feet." Then S-T-O-P. No seriously, don't say anything else unless a different question is asked.

- **Ask questions back.** People learn by asking questions. Instead of being the font of all knowledge (FOAK) for your child, start putting her in the driver's seat. When we include kids by asking for their thoughts and opinions, they learn to trust themselves. Here is where you might ask, "Why do you think you have to wear your boots?" This might take awhile before your child takes the bait, especially if he's in a foul humor, but at some point he'll generate a conversation about what he thinks. You might find you learn a lot.

- **Reflect.** At the end of the day, look for patterns. What topics were difficult for you to answer simply? How did *Answer the Question Asked* change the conversation between you and your child? I bet you'll find that your talks became more child-centered and less about you. What do you think about that?

A BLUEPRINT FOR FULL IMPLEMENTATION

Step 1: Using your PRN (Parent Resource Notebook), write down big conversation topics.

Besides taking care of these small, helpless bodies and keeping them safe, imparting information is arguably one of the most important tasks of being a parent. Check out Template #4 for one example and a place to write your own. You are going to write down big conversation topics in your PRN. Here are some examples:

- Is nighttime scary?

- Why do people get married?

- Is it okay to be different?

- What is sex?

- Is there a heaven?

- Is Santa real?

- What happens after we die?

- What is divorce?

Step 2: Talk to supportive people.

This is where your online or in-real-life parent friends are going to come in handy. Even if your kids seem extra inquisitive, chances are other parents have answered the same questions your kids are asking. You will find no shortage of parents out there who want to share how they talked about the big things with their children. When your kids were little, you probably didn't care about hearing these conversations, but when your kids ask the first big question, the tide shifts. I can't get enough of hearing about how other parents tackle big topics. Every once in awhile someone tells me something genius about how they handled a sticky parenting question, and I am forever grateful.

Step 3: Be prepared with some standard answers.

Literally write down some of your answers in your PRN. Don't assume you will remember what you think about these big topics in the moment. If your child asks you an important question and you don't feel prepared, ask to chat with her later about it. But make sure you keep your appointment to talk. Later in the book we'll talk about Mantra 7: *Honesty Comes with Trust,* but for now just remember that they trust you because they know you'll tell them the truth. You have to give it to them so they'll keep coming back. This means that you need to stop at nothing to find the information and develop a way to share this with your child. Sometimes picture books can be incredibly helpful in opening the doors to a conversation. There are lots of social-emotional picture books out there for almost any topic: Google them. When you are ready, let your child know and then *Answer the Question Asked.*

Step 4: Give simple bits of information until your child seems satisfied, then S-T-O-P.

This is definitely the hardest part of this mantra and the most important. Though you are excited to share how baby Juniper came into this world, your child may not be ready to hear about it. If she asks you where Juniper came from, she may not want to learn more than, "My tummy." Consider the question asked. If she really wants to know more, she'll ask a deeper question like, "How did a baby get in your tummy?" Even with that question, though, she might only be ready to hear that the dad has a seed that gets planted in the mom's egg. Wait for all the questions to come up before you go down the birds and bees route. Take note: This is also a time to make sure you aren't undermining their questioning in the way you answer. Using sarcasm is rarely appropriate for children, yet we do it regularly.

When adults give children too much information, they can feel frightened. Frightened children keep feelings inside and tend to think situations are scarier than they really are. The simpler we are in our answers and reactions, the more likely children are to trust us enough to be honest with us. Learning to *Answer the Question Asked* is transformative for both child and parent.

OVERCOMING PUSHBACK

This appears to be a very simple mantra, but you can expect a few barriers. Here are ways to hurdle them:

I think kids should be informed. If I don't answer the question in full now, it may never come up again. Make no bones about it, I am a strong advocate for telling kids the truth, but being a grownup means you've lived longer and experienced more. It also means you process information differently. You understand that knowing things does not make them more likely to happen. Not so true with children. The minute they learn about things, they think it's going to happen to them. It's a developmental fact. While children need to have their questions answered, they do not need to know everything all at once. The questions will always come back up as the child needs the answers. The important thing to remember here is that you want your child to come back to a reliable source. If you give too much information now, your child is likely to tune out, or worse—stop coming to you altogether—and who knows how Johnny down the street is going to explain it later. Be a simple, reliable source for your children.

What if my child is too shy to ask questions? This is a very valid pushback. There has been some research that shows children's questions are a necessary part of their cognitive development. If this is true, then you must help your child gather up the courage and confidence to ask a question or two. The only way I know to do this is through trust and patience. Never belittle the child or make fun of his questions. Make every tiny step in the direction of a question be a point of celebration, much in the same way you celebrated when your son (or daughter) said Mama or Dada or rolled over for the first time. Then whenever a question is asked, answer it as simply as possible. This will open the door to more questions.

There is so much I have to share with my child and the time goes by so quickly. What's that thing they say about childhood? The days are long, but the years are short. Yes, that's it. It's true that the time goes by quickly, but we can no more pack everything we've ever wanted to say and do into eighteen years than we can stuff memories in a jar for later. The best part about answering the question asked is that it forces you to be present in the moment. We can only do the best we can in the space we've got. More than likely, you'll get your chance to say what you want to say, eventually. I won't lie and say that life is never too short, but I will tell you that one simple day with your child, answering his questions, will make it a better life.

What if my child shares her new knowledge with her friends, who aren't ready to hear the information? Your responsibility is to your own children, so answer the questions your children ask. If you feel the information might be something not everyone would share with their kids, you can always let your kids know to be careful with whom they share it. Will they share their new knowledge with their friends? They might, but if the information is accurate and easy for that age group to digest, it should be okay. You really cannot prepare for every other child's eventuality.

THE MANTRA IN ACTION

"What's a period?" my ten-year-old son asked from the back seat.

"What do you mean? The dot at the end of a sentence?" I responded. I take *Answer the Question Asked* very seriously.

"No, it's something to do with girls. Here's the thing. I guess there's a talk at the end of fifth grade, but I missed it and now I feel stupid because everyone knows and I don't."

Fair enough. We were in the car with my nine-year-old daughter headed to the mall, so I figured now was as good a time as any to discuss puberty.

In the fifteen seconds of space between my son's question and my commitment to *Answer the Question Asked*, my brain raced through what I'd written in my PRN. I remembered that my husband and I had decided (though he prayed it would be me) they needed:

1. The truth

2. The question being asked to be answered

3. The time to connect in many ways

4. An ability to shut down to process

5. The knowledge that it's okay if they decide not to pursue it further

Then I launched right into answering the question. "A period," I said, "is when a girl's body begins to bleed from her vagina. It happens once a month starting around age eleven or twelve."

"Oh," my son said.

"What?!" my daughter said.

"Do they get to take the day off from school?" my son asked.

"We wish," I laughed, "but no. It's not that bad."

The conversation went on in a fairly question-and-answer sort of format. Then, the connections changed course.

"Why would a girl get her period when she was eleven if that made her body ready to have a baby?" my son questioned.

"Well, technically I guess she could get pregnant at eleven," I said.

And then there were crickets. My son went back to his iPhone, my daughter back to reading. I knew the conversation would come back, but for now it was over. Go me.

Answer the Question Asked doesn't require a list of parenting resources or special programs, though some will be helpful in gathering your thoughts. It really just needs you to be present, honest, and careful with your words. It is awesome that these days parents feel free to communicate about important topics with their children, but this does not mean that children are ready for adult conversations. *Answer the Question Asked* and stay in the moment. Your children will grow and make connections that generate new questions.

MANTRA 5

HUNGRY. ANGRY. LONELY. TIRED. (H.A.L.T.)

Tend to Basic Needs Before Making Assumptions

Whoever travels without a guide needs two hundred years for a two-day journey.
— RUMI

THE PROBLEM: PUNISHING A CHILD FOR THE SMALLER PICTURE

IF YOU'RE A parent, you've been there: that moment you realize your child is melting down because she is starving, not spoiled. Here you'd been putting her in a timeout and agonizing over why this was happening to you in the middle of a store, when suddenly you noticed it was 1:30 p.m. and you had forgotten to serve lunch. It happens, forgive yourself. We forget that basic needs must be met before we can teach someone something.

Abraham Maslow was an American psychologist who is best known for creating Maslow's hierarchy of needs. In his theory, there is an order of basic human needs that must be met before a person can develop his identity. In Maslow's model, physiological stuff is at the bottom, indicating the needs that must be met first before others can be met. The basic needs are breathing, food, water, sex, sleep, homeostasis, and excretion. The next level up is safety, then love and belonging, then esteem, and finally self-actualization. If you're trying to teach your child higher-order needs, be sure you've covered the lower ones first. If you'd like a visual of these needs, do a Google search for Maslow's hierarchy of needs, and click on images.

I subscribe to this theory because I have seen it in action over and over as both a parent and a teacher. When I had kids come to school without breakfast, they didn't function well until I got them something to eat. Who cares about the alphabet when your parents are getting divorced and you're angry, or for that matter, when you're hungry?

> It is nothing short of miraculous to watch the calm that occurs when a basic need is met.

The thing we forget the most and the thing that will bring us closer to our kids is that basic needs must be met first. It doesn't matter how much planning goes into your parenting if you aren't stopping to draw your child near and learn what they need physically and emotionally in that moment.

THE MANTRA: HUNGRY. ANGRY. LONELY. TIRED. (H.A.L.T.)

The key to parenting well is a combination of care and awareness. By taking care of your child and recognizing certain signs, you can prevent many tantrums, misunderstandings, and frustrations. The mantra is *H.A.L.T.* This helpful acronym reminds you to take a moment and ask yourself if your child is feeling hungry, angry, lonely, or tired. It seems simple enough, but when these basic needs are not met, no reminders can be heard. Fortunately, hunger, anger, loneliness, and tiredness can be easy to address and serve as a warning system before things reach a breaking point.

When we make it a practice to stop, assess, and take care of basic needs, we teach our children to do the same. It is a proven fact that people who do not recognize basic need signals find other ways of feeling better. These are the kids who end up obese, alcoholic, and addicted to drugs. As children, these basic needs are all-consuming. If you've ever witnessed a complete meltdown by your child three minutes before dinner is served, you know what I'm talking about.

Hunger is a physical need. Understanding the need to eat is fairly straightforward. However, you must remind yourself not just to get your child food, but to feed her well. Meeting nutritional needs allows children's bodies to operate at the highest potential, and will keep your child feeling better.

Anger is a normal, healthy emotion to experience. The important thing is to H.A.L.T. and take time to understand what is causing his anger, and make sure he knows how to properly express it. This takes time and patience. Children are allowed to be childish, but parents must maintain their cool and help their child through the anger.

Loneliness can occur when we are by ourselves or when surrounded by many people. Children have little control over their lives, so loneliness or feeling unsafe can happen at times when adults least expect it. Be on the lookout for signs of loneliness when you are at a restaurant, party, or (quite frankly) any place other than home following a typical routine. Children often feel lonely just because the routine has been changed. They act out, seek attention, and otherwise behave in ways you'll wish no one was witness to.

Tiredness takes a toll on body, mind, and spirit. When we fill children's days with activities, we think we are helping them. However, running low on energy compromises their ability to think and their capacity to cope. It's also critical for children to have at least ten hours of sleep. This means that you need to watch the clock to help manage their time. Remember to start things much earlier than when you expect your child to complete them. Asking your child to get ready for bed five minutes after bedtime is not something you want to get in a regular habit of doing.

WHAT YOU CAN DO TOMORROW

- **Review the mantra H.A.L.T.** These four basic needs will be present throughout any part of one day. Look for them. This is a mantra you'll want to say to yourself regularly. It'll help you calm down when your child appears irrational or is stopping you from accomplishing anything. I have been known to say *Hungry, Angry, Lonely, Tired* under my breath over and over until it suddenly dawns on me which one of these needs has not been met.

- **Become a basic needs coach.** Say something like this, "I can see that you are hungry. Let's go get something to eat." If your child is anything like mine, she may freak out at this point, insisting she is not hungry. But, you will either bring her to the kitchen or hand her a banana. Like *Answer the Question Asked* or *Begin at the End*, this mantra makes sense and works so beautifully when you use it simply. Use Template #5 to identify ways to solve these needs so you'll have them in your toolbox as they arise.

- **Notice the immediate shift that occurs.** It is nothing short of miraculous to watch the calm that occurs when a basic need is met. Remember this; you'll need this coaching memory throughout the day. It might help you to take a picture of the before and after of *Hungry, Angry, Lonely, Tired.* I know many people might frown if you take out your iPhone while your child is having a tantrum, but it's for the good of the order, right? Plus, sometimes you're just sitting around waiting it out anyway, at least until you figure out what need is going unmet. Take a picture of the insanity and then use your new coaching skill. Then take a happy picture. Keep these pictures. Review them. You need to commit them to your memory so you can mentally retrieve them in the next moment of insanity.

- **State the problem and solution for your child.** "Look at that, you were upset during the game, but then we remembered you hadn't eaten. You were just hungry! You ate a banana and now you feel

63

> better. Now, let's go back to the game and see if
> you can beat me!" This helps her see the connec-
> tions between how we perform and how we feel
> and shows her a way to take care of her needs. I can
> think of lots of adults in my life who I wish had this
> kind of *H.A.L.T.* training as children.

A BLUEPRINT FOR FULL IMPLEMENTATION

Step 1: Label emotions for your child.

Throughout the day, label and discuss the emotions you see your child going through. "Wow, you were tired!" or "Being angry is normal and important. Can you tell me what made you so angry?" As you get better at this, you might consider adding other emotions to your conversations. Most adults tell people they are: "fine," "great," "okay," or "not great." These words don't tell us very much. In fact, they can also be used as a way to hide our emotions. In order to cope with the emotion your child feels, it must first be identified. In fact, when an emotion is identified and labeled, it becomes easier for a person to manage.

Step 2: Establish ways of solving each basic need.

These basic needs pop up through the day for all human beings. We have to learn to deal with them or we begin to get our needs met in less appropriate ways. Help your child learn techniques for solving basic needs. This would be a great time to take out your PRN and jot down ways to solve basic needs. While your child is young, you will be meeting these basic needs, but as he gets older, you want him to recognize and take care of his needs himself, when possible. Remind yourself and your child about the mantra *Hungry, Angry, Lonely, Tired*, and sear it into your brain so you won't forget to use it. This caring, teaching mode is called parenting, right? That's what makes it so tough. We need to see it, solve it, and discuss what we did so our child can learn from it.

Step 3: Create and post an anchor chart.

Teachers have great luck with anchor charts, so it makes sense to borrow this technique from the classroom. An anchor chart is a tool to help with self-regulation and support independence. It is visual evidence of the work that your child practices. Anchor charts are temporary by nature, so once your child (and you) learns to keep *H.A.L.T.* concepts in mind and use them regularly, you can throw away the anchor chart.

Hungry	Keep regular eating times, have snacks with you, make healthy choices
Angry	Quiet yourself, breathe, say "I am angry because ..." and "I need ..."
Lonely	Reach out for someone, ask for a hug, start a conversation
Tired	Keep regular sleeping times, take a nap, do a quiet activity

OVERCOMING PUSHBACK

No matter how obvious this mantra appears, people will always find a way to tell you to do something different when you are in the midst of a chaotic parenting situation. They want to be nice, but you can be secure in knowing that the *H.A.L.T.* mantra works in the moment and is a preventive strategy. Here are the most likely arguments you might hear:

You're just going to let her get away with that? There are so many moments in parenting when you must choose the lesson to teach. It is a long-term strategy to teach your child the lesson that basic needs must come first. Tell these pushbackers that you are trying to raise a person who is self-aware instead of responsive to everyone else's requests. No one ever regretted learning the tools of personal care and safety, but often people regret not knowing how to set their own boundaries.

The party just got started and you're already leaving? There are many sacrifices we make as parents. The key is to prioritize. If you know that your child can make your life a living hell when she is tired, and that she never sleeps in late in the morning, then you should leave the party early. If, however, you have a child who enjoys the nighttime activities and will sleep in the next morning, then stay at the party because your child will still get enough sleep. It's your choice.

In my day, we ate three meals a day. While three meals a day with no snacks may be great for some kids, others need to regulate their blood sugar more often. Carry snacks. Make them nutritious. You know your child best and you are the one who will have to deal with the consequences of a hungry child if you aren't prepared.

You should put her in timeout. Studies have shown that "time-in" can be more effective in combatting behaviors triggered by feeling angry or lonely. It's not easy being a kid, and the isolation of timeout can be the most terrifying of propositions, leading to worse behavior. A hug from someone who loves them may solve the situation best in the moment, and help prevent it in the future!

THE MANTRA IN ACTION

We have to be careful observers of our children in order to identify what is going on when something seems different. We can help prevent or lessen a meltdown by paying attention to their behavior and using the mantra *H.A.L.T.* to check their basic needs.

Emily Popek, mother of one, says, "Once, my daughter woke up from her nap and was absolutely beside herself with rage. She was incoherently screaming, kicking her legs, wouldn't let me touch her. She was so unhinged that it was actually frightening to me, especially since I had NO IDEA what had triggered it. Finally, it dawned on me that she had basically skipped lunch, and was probably very hungry. I ran downstairs and brought her a spoonful of yogurt to eat right there in her bed! Within minutes she seemed to be "herself" again. Versions of this scenario have repeated several times, but now at least I can spot the problem a little quicker, and get her something to help with her blood sugar."

Sometimes we also have to check in with ourselves when things feel different and not okay with us as parents. After all, we have basic needs too!

Elizabeth Pagel-Hogan, parent of two, shares, "One day this summer, I had just completed a workout, then I rushed into the shower. I was crazed trying to get kids out the door for appointments. As soon as we were buckled, I went into a yelling-about-cleaning rage as I backed our minivan out of the driveway. 'All you do is leave messes for other people to clean up and if you want to hire a maid these are my rates, but I can't be a maid and a mom!' I yelled. My oldest, twelve, said, 'Mom, I'm not trying to backtalk. And I know we need to clean up. But it's almost 2 p.m., you did a workout, and I didn't see you eat lunch. That might be making you feel on edge.' And he was right."

Taking care goes both ways. Everyone needs to *H.A.L.T.* and check in to see if the current chaos could be resolved with food, soothing, comfort, or sleep.

H.A.L.T. can serve as a reminder to all of us that we need to take care of our basic needs every day. It is one of the easiest, instantly successful parenting steps to take—reaping benefits long after our children are grown. Taking the time to center oneself and focus on needs is a skill that people have sought after for hundreds of years. Practice it yourself, and teach your children to tune in to their own basic needs first.

THE PRIZE IS IN THE PROCESS

Allow for Thinking Time

There is a way between voice and presence,
where information flows. In disciplined silence
it opens; with wandering talk it closes.
— RUMI

THE PROBLEM: WE DON'T GIVE CHILDREN ENOUGH TIME

THERE ARE TWO ways to look at this problem. One is that we don't give children enough time to consider everything they know and connect that knowledge to the request or question being asked. This is a lot to ask of someone, really. Two is that we only value the end result of something. The process of figuring something out is not straightforward and can seem like a waste of time. How you connect to something and make it a part of your vernacular likely is quite different from the way your child develops his knowledge.

I can't tell you how many times I have said things like, "Seriously? What don't you understand about: Put your clothes in the hamper?" This is no way to help someone learn. Just because a person doesn't understand exactly what I mean when I say something, doesn't mean she can't learn it. It does mean I have to model it better or give her time to think about it.

Oftentimes we parents make the mistake of taking silence for understanding, or lack of caring. Sometimes silence means your child is:

- Still thinking about what you said

- Angry and has tuned out

- Confused and is wondering what to say or do next

The thing about process is that it's different for everyone and it has nothing to do with intelligence. Processing speed is the pace at which you take in information, make sense of it, and begin to respond. This information can be visual, such as letters and numbers. It can also be auditory, such as spoken language. When you ask kids questions or give them information, they must take in those words and connect the new information to already learned information. Sometimes it happens instantly, but more often than not it takes a bit of time to process. If we only value and reward the answer they generate, then we miss the point of being human. Children need to know that the work they do, the thinking they do, and the questions they ask are the point. The answers help them move along in the process, but *The Prize Is in the Process.*

THE MANTRA: THE PRIZE IS IN THE PROCESS

We need to show kids how important the process is by modeling and talking about it out loud. This is called "making thinking visible," or sharing our metacognition. We make thinking visible when we create routine processes for children. They are the patterns by which we go about the job of learning and working together. A routine is a process that is used repeatedly to accomplish goals. Households have routine processes designed to manage children's behavior, to organize, and to communicate. Routines also help structure the way children go about the process of learning. When we show kids that there is a process to follow, we help them understand that *The Prize Is in the Process.*

Consider this: If kids think all you want them to do is have a laundry hamper in the room, they aren't getting the point that process is the valued skill. You must show them how to scan their bedrooms for loose items of clothing and talk it through as you go. "Oh, look, there's a shirt here that needs to be washed. Mom can find it better if I put it in the hamper for her." Or, "When I put everything in the hamper, it's all in one place for when I need to get my clothes cleaned." *The Prize Is in the Process* because life is easier when we follow a routine. It makes sense instead of seeming unpredictable.

It may seem silly to do this, but the reality is that just because an adult sees the process laid out in front of him when he thinks, "I want clean clothes for next week," a child does not think this way. Children have not experienced this process enough to make it their own. Think about creating experiences for your child instead of teaching her lessons. You aren't teaching her to wash her clothes. You're teaching her the entire process that starts with removing clean clothes from her drawers, wearing them, and then taking off the dirty clothes—through every action that gets those same clothes back in her drawer clean again.

When people learn to appreciate process, they can start to generalize the experience. For example, a child who knows to look for clothes that might need cleaning and get them into the right bin may also begin to see the similarities in looking for dishes that belong in a sink, or looking for books that need to be in a backpack for the next day. Moving a child from doing a task to understanding a process is a turning point. When you feel rushed and frustrated that your child isn't accomplishing or learning a task fast enough, repeat the mantra, *The Prize Is in the Process*. You will become a better teacher for your child, and eventually your child will begin to design processes to accomplish goals. Wow!

> **When we allow for thinking time and prize the process, we send kids the message that daily life is worth doing well.**

WHAT YOU CAN DO TOMORROW

- **Explain why and how.** We get really good at saying the "what" about chores, but we forget the importance of the "why" and "how." If we don't supply our rationale, children are likely to be defiant. Just as we don't like doing things that seem purposeless, neither do they. It's much easier for them to handle putting a bike away in the garage when they know someone might run over it in the driveway. Plus, it's awesome to find your bike in the same place every time you want to ride.

- **Identify one clean-up or organizing process to work on.** We've already learned not to give our kids too much to work on at a time. This is another of those times when you must take it slowly. Choose one clean-up or organizing process that you think your child is ready to learn. You might identify this by recalling that thing that raises your blood pressure every. single. time. For me, it's cleaning up after my kids have made an art mess. For you, it might be a different process.

- **Practice what you preach.** This isn't going to work if you aren't modeling the process. If you spend your time agonizing over putting away your cooking supplies, you aren't showing them the value of the process. The prize within the process is that work is accomplished and you get better at it each time you practice it.

- **Make sure your kids have what they need.** They need to know what the area looks like when it is clean. They need to know where the right tools are to clean the area. Help them out with that part until they understand that part of the process is locating the right tools.

- **Praise them during the process.** This is a critical difference. We parents have gotten used to telling kids what to do and then telling them not to bother us until they are finished. This only reinforces that the process is lonely and long. Instead, cheer them on while they clean. Tell them how great it is that some of the glitter got in the dust pan. Let them toss some of the glue sticks into a bin to see if they make it. The process doesn't have to be grueling. They might laugh at you, but this will end up feeling less like something to get through and more like family time. *The Prize Is in the Process.*

A BLUEPRINT FOR FULL IMPLEMENTATION

Using the same process that artists, scientists, and lawyers use to identify problems and locate solutions in a step-by-step manner will help kids whenever a problem comes up—so, like every other hour.

Step 1: Identify the challenges before you meet with your child(ren).

What are you asking your child to do? You need to explain exactly what the final result will look like. Sometimes it can be extremely helpful for kids to see an example of what you'd like the result to be—plan to provide it. Check out Template #6 to see an example and a template to plan a challenge of your own. The first thing you must do, though, is state the challenge. The challenge we'll use as an example is: My child will take a shower completely independently.

Step 2: Brainstorm.

The word brainstorm has a very parenting-related origin. At the end of the 19th century, people used the term brainstorm to describe a mental disturbance. Can you see the parenting connection now? I don't think I've had a complete uninterrupted thought since my first child was born. Over time, of course, the term has shifted from a problem to sharing ideas. Ask your kids to help you solve the problem or challenge. Tell them about a problem of your own. No, really, share a problem, but with discretion, of course.

Tell them that as a member of a family, you need to know that your children can manage to clean themselves completely without you. Tell them that just like doing their homework and not losing their iPhones, you are the manager of lots of different details. Each one requires a process that makes them easier to accomplish. Let them know that your parenting plan involves them taking on some of these things—in particular, a shower—so that you don't have to do all the work all the time. Also, explain that someday they will be responsible for all of these details and you want them to be prepared. The point is not just to get clean, but *The Prize Is in the Process* of learning to keep oneself clean.

Step 3: Develop each process.

The more you do this together with your kids, the faster you'll see results. The truth is that we don't really think about all the processes involved in being a person, and that's why we parents get so mad when something that seems easy to accomplish isn't being done. This is truly the reason I started writing this book. I was aware of three mothers who fell apart when their freshmen in college dropped out because being independent was too overwhelming. This seemed so sad to me.

These kids literally couldn't figure out how to manage without someone telling them how to do each process that made up a daily life. They only felt like they couldn't reach the thing they considered to be the prize: the good grades. In fact, if they understood how valuable the process was, they may have felt less unsure. The more processes you develop together, the more likely they are to see how many processes are like templates for seemingly unrelated things. Once your child learns how to do everything that taking a shower involves, he may eventually see how similar this is to cleaning anything from the dog to his new car.

Step 4: Test and evaluate each process.

This is where the rubber meets the road. All talk and no action is not a good parenting strategy. We need to include kids in the test and evaluation phase so they can see how their ideas pan out. It may be that one (or all) of your kids needs a chart to remember how the process works. Do this! Use a template for a comic strip and have your child draw each part of the process. Don't do it for him. The goal is to gain knowledge of how processing works, so if you do this part your child may not make the leap to do it on her own.

Step 5: Rebuild if necessary.

What if it turns out that your child's use of only one soap for shampoo, conditioner, face cleaner, and body wash isn't working? Bring your kids together and go back to Step 2. It might be a five-second fix, like, "Hey, that soap is leaving residue in your hair. How 'bout you use a different product for each purpose, and keep them all in a rack attached to the wall shower?" Okay!

OVERCOMING PUSHBACK

Some parents believe they should do it all. Those parents are wrong. Ha! Parenthood is about learning too. We have to learn that we are facilitating the process of a child moving into adulthood. Your mantra here is *The Prize Is in the Process.* Say it to yourself over and over until it feels good to you. You are giving kids prizes when you have them learn about the process. Really—you are. This is that whole "Don't give him a fish, teach him to fish" thing.

Some things are so easy to do, why go through this trouble? Model everything, assume nothing. Just because you know the process of going to the bathroom doesn't mean your youngster knows all the steps in that process: close and lock the door, turn a light on, pull your pants down but not off, sit on a toilet, take out just the right amount of toilet paper, wipe without getting anything on you but make sure you are clean, stand up, flush, pull up your pants, make sure your zipper is closed, wash your hands with both soap and water, and dry them. Modeling a process, and giving children plenty of time to learn it, will actually help them to accomplish it faster!

If we teach every kid that *The Prize Is in the Process*, isn't that the same as giving everyone a trophy? No, and everyone doesn't need a trophy in the real world. Lots of people get by just fine without being number one, two, or three at something they've accomplished. However, everyone does need to know how to accomplish goals they set, and the best way to do that is by following a process. Consider incentives and rewards when they follow a process and reach a goal.

I don't have time to do this with every process for each of my children. Carefully planning processes to teach your child does take time. However, this time investment is time well spent when you are working on something in the kitchen and you realize your kids are showering, doing the laundry, or vacuuming their rooms without you.

THE MANTRA IN ACTION

There is no shortage of ways to teach about process, so it's kind of amazing that it gets so much pushback. Taking care of the details of life can be complicated and overwhelming.

Bonnie Smith raised her daughter Yvette mostly on her own. For her, teaching the concept of process was important. She says parents tend to skip it and then wonder why a kid or teen doesn't intuitively know the process that goes along with the request to "Do the dishes," for example. So Bonnie modeled how to rinse the sink, put leftovers into containers, wipe down counters, push in chairs at the dinner table, etc.

"My parenting focus has always been about the creative process, not product. Whatever outcome that resulted was secondary to what she learned in the process to get there. I'm a big proponent of this type of experiential learning: research/explore, make informed decisions, take action, reflect, and adjust as needed. My biggest takeaway and lesson learned long-term was empowering her with tools to take ownership of her own decisions and choices and to trust her internal compass."

Bonnie says, "When my daughter and I took a college tour, I coached her through the planning process. She had to plan, look at distances, and contact the colleges to sign up for tours. I was there, of course, to guide and show her tools, answer questions, and give input, but in the end it was her college tour. It would have been easier to do it myself but she loved the tour and got more out of it because she owned the process."

We often think of childhood as having an end result of becoming an adult, but the process of childhood is the important part—the prize. It's what's learned along the way that will help our children when they are adults. Use your parenting skills to shine a light on the importance of process. When we allow for thinking time and prize the process, we send kids the message that daily life is worth doing well.

MANTRA 7

HONESTY COMES WITH TRUST

Build Relationships with Children

Out beyond ideas of wrongdoing and rightdoing,
there is a field. I'll meet you there.
— RUMI

THE PROBLEM: SOMETIMES CHILDREN LIE

ABOVE ALL ELSE, parents tell me they wish their children wouldn't lie. I often hear them say, "I can't trust him if he lies!" Dishonesty is an inherent part of being a human being because we are capable of knowing that it's possible to have a consequence for every action. Therefore, we want to avoid what might happen if someone knows the truth. Even young children can figure out that lying to cover up the truth may be the lesser risk. It might be frustrating to parents, but it makes good survival sense.

Pathological lying isn't considered a psychologically clinical diagnosis, but merely a symptom of something else. Children never lie because something is wrong with them; rather something is broken in the system.

There are a few basic reasons children lie:

> **The more kids see that a solution is a better choice than a lie, the more they will solve problems.**

- The lie feels like it matters to them.

- Telling the truth feels like giving up control.

- They don't want to disappoint you.

- Lies snowball.

- It's not a lie to them.

- They want it to be true.

Studies show that more than ninety-five percent of all kids lie regularly by the age of six. It's a way of testing out boundaries and how their parents will react. You can either show them you care or you can shut them out.

THE MANTRA: HONESTY COMES WITH TRUST

Though parents think the cycle starts with a child being honest and ends with a parent trusting them, it's really the reverse. When a child feels trusted, he will begin to be honest. This means it all starts with the parent. Trust grows through relationship-building. You need to build trust so that your interests are aligned. Children inherently want to please their parents, but situations force them to begin lying as a way of surviving. Psychologically, the best way to get someone to be honest with you is to get her to see that you both are similar. The more similar a person feels to someone else, the more empathetic they are to the other person. This empathy increases willingness to trust the other person as well.

Being similar is not as difficult as it may appear. As humans, we are all similar. Once you take this tact with your child, you will find that she begins to empathize with you almost immediately. Stop saying, "You need to do this ..." and start saying, "When I do this..." Studies have shown that people who see themselves as similar to another person in how they respond to music are more likely to help the other person out. Researchers put two people in a room and played music through two sets of headphones. Each person was supposed to tap out the beat. For some people, the music was the same; for others the music was different. When people saw that the person across from them was tapping the same way, they were more likely to help the other person later when the person asked for assistance. Isn't that fascinating? But how can we use that with our children? When we follow the mantra, *Honesty Comes with Trust*, we need to remember that building trust is always the first step.

WHAT **YOU** CAN DO TOMORROW

Try out musical tapping with a younger child:

- **Put on some music.** Find a song you and your child like to listen to together. Make sure it's a song where the beat changes from a slow to a fast tempo quite regularly. Try using classical music where the lyrics aren't competing with the music.

- **Ask your child to tap to the music.** If you don't regularly listen to music, you might have to show your child how to tap to the beat. It won't be long before the two of you are happily tapping away.

- **Smile as you tap.** This is supposed to be a time for encouraging trust and similarities. So show your joy, and you might even want to exaggerate it a bit.

- **Talk about your experience.** What did you find easy? What did you find difficult? Were you always in sync? This is a simple way to start feeling how important modeling is for your child.

Try taking a class with an older child to learn something neither of you knows how to do:

- **Ask your teen what he'd like to learn.** Talk about how learning new things is such a great way to figure out what you are good at and what you enjoy.

- **Look up nearby or online courses.** Do it together. Find a class that teaches yoga or rock climbing or fly tying and sign up together.

- **Share your struggles.** Talk about the new thing you are learning. What do you find easy? What do you find difficult? Were you always in sync?

A BLUEPRINT FOR FULL IMPLEMENTATION

Step 1: Find similarities throughout your day.

Your job is to look for the similarities between you and your child. At first, you might just notice them without saying anything. Perhaps you both are right-handed. You both love to eat bacon on Saturday morning. You are both driven by a need to be outdoors. Take a look at Template #7 to see what characteristics to look for. After you've noticed these traits, start to mention them in unobtrusive ways. "That was exactly what I was going to order! I wonder why we both wanted it?" And "Wow, we both like to spend time outdoors. I'm happy we're so alike!"

These similarities will start to become part of the story of you and your child. Stories play a vital role in the growth and development of children. When you and your child create positive memories that can be retold as family stories, you build a trusting relationship. With the *Honesty Comes with Trust* mantra, a trusting relationship is the key to your children telling you the truth. They already know your story and they know how you will react to them—with love and respect—because you see yourself in your child.

Step 2: Introduce things by sharing your similarities.

Now that you've discovered how much you have in common with your child and he is starting to notice the same, make it a point to state similarities whenever you need him to do something. "You know how we both agonize over getting our work done? I've been finding lately that when I set a timer I can get a lot more done than I thought. Try doing your homework that way." This sounds much less controlling to a child than, "Set a timer when you do your homework."

Step 3: Talk about lying.

Many parents make the mistake of not talking about things. It's easy to feel like a child should know the difference between a lie and the truth, but they don't … at first. This is a great place to share how you feel when you lie and how you feel when someone else lies to you. Be sure to discuss the different reasons lying is not acceptable as a choice. From the lack of safety to the loss of trust, lying is likely to be something that separates you from your child many times in the future. This is also a great time to talk about problem-solving. Much of the reason that kids lie is because they don't know how to solve the problem at hand. Give your child a way out. Explain that when they come to you with the truth and an idea for solving the issue, you will be more likely to stay calm. The more kids see that a solution is a better choice than a lie, the more they will solve problems. *Honesty Comes with Trust*; it just does.

Step 4: Work on trust every day.

Trust is not something that can be introduced and then left alone. Every time we do anything with our children, we have the opportunity to build trust or tear it down. The great news is that every day is a new day for building trust. Find your similarities and share them with your child because the more she sees that you are similar, the more likely she is to tell you the truth. She knows she wouldn't want to be lied to and you seem just the same.

OVERCOMING PUSHBACK

Are you going to tell your child that since you lie too, it's okay?
When you tell people that you are building trust by sharing similarities, this is likely to come up as a pushback. The truth is that you are going to have to share that you have lied and that you continue

to lie. We all lie about things. We even label some of them "white" lies in order to make ourselves feel better about them. It's not okay to lie, but sometimes it might be necessary, right? This is why it's so tough to teach a child about not lying. Do your best and let kids know that you, too, are not perfect.

You are not your child's friend; you are the parent. When people see that you are working on building trust through finding similarities, they may think that you are becoming BFFs with your child. Finding similarities in the human experience is not the same as being best friends because you both love cotton candy. You are going to show that the way you experience life as a person is very similar to the way your child experiences life. When we recognize how alike we all are, we begin to break down the walls of mistrust. When we establish that we can be trusted, our children will be honest with us.

Lying is a sin. Note: You are never going to say it's okay to lie. You are merely going to say that it's sometimes hard not to lie. This opens up the lines of communication to share something that will likely happen with your child. If your child thinks that you have never lied in your life, then he is unlikely to come to you when he commits this now unpardonable sin. The goal is to get your child to come to you with a solution in mind instead of a lie waiting to be told.

THE MANTRA IN ACTION

Instead of writing about lying in action, which we've all seen, I'm going to share a story about trust in action. When Chloe was in college and on a lacrosse team, she felt caught between doing what was right for herself and what was considered loyal behavior by the team.

They wanted her to drink alcohol at parties, but she had signed a team document saying she wouldn't drink as a team member.

How could she justify it? Instead of feeling alone in this decision, Chloe knew there was someone she could go to—her mother, Cathi. They had built a relationship based on trust. She called her mom up and told her the situation. Her mother didn't act horrified that Chloe was contemplating drinking at a party with her new teammates, because getting angry and acting surprised was not a way to help Chloe with her problem. They talked about the situation and Chloe made a decision to speak with her coach. The issue was deep because the coach did not know that this was going on and the captain was fostering the drinking plan. Chloe felt like she was caught between a rock and a hard place. She had been there before.

Back in high school another drinking incident had occurred, and Chloe had made a decision to lie to her parents. She had been punished for the incident by her parents because she was underage and they wanted her to understand that drinking was an adult decision. They didn't act like she was a bad person for behaving a certain way, but they did give her an appropriate consequence. And years later, Chloe thought about that learning experience, and she decided she could trust her parents again to give her advice, rather than anger.

After talking with the lacrosse coach, Chloe faced some challenging fallout. Her teammates began ostracizing her. She needed her mom more than ever this time, and Cathi stepped in again. Together, they made a decision to move Chloe to a new college and a new team where she is very happy. The trust between Chloe and her mother led to a discussion, a good decision, and peace of mind.

Building trust into your relationship is one of those parenthood processes that requires stamina and intentional thinking. We can't build a foundation in one day. It's not something that happens once and then just works. The stronger your foundation of trust, the less likely lying will infiltrate your lives. Kids who trust that their parents will be helpful and kind because they are empathetic are the ones who come to their parents when it really matters. Be that parent whenever you get the chance because *Honesty Comes with Trust.*

MANTRA 8

LET MY DECISION STAND

Say It Once and Mean It Whenever Possible

There is a voice that doesn't use words. Listen.
— RUMI

THE PROBLEM: WE REPEAT THE SAME THING
OR CHANGE WHAT WE'RE SAYING

I HAVE TO ADMIT that I first came across this mantra concept when I was training seeing eye dogs. None of us were professional trainers; we were all just volunteers hoping to do our best, which is a lot like how parenting feels—right? (Friendly disclaimer: I am *not* saying raising children is akin to training dogs. This is simply a principle I was able to extrapolate.) The trainer told us that it was important for a blind person not to end up with a dog who only listens when he feels like it. Dogs who learn that you will say a command more than once will wait until you give the command in such a way that they must respond. Sound familiar?

Here's how this concept has played out in my own life. When I was little, my brothers and I discovered that my mother's first request was not the end of the line. It wasn't until she was nearly hysterical that we would decide to do what she asked. I've found this is true of many requests. Why would anyone do something unless they really had to or they wanted to?

Here's an example (though I doubt you need one): Five minutes ago you asked Grace to bring her plate into the kitchen. You ask her again, but this time you sound irritated. "Yup, one second." Five minutes later, you say, "What did you not understand about 'Bring your plate into the kitchen?' I hate when you do this. Why can't you just pick up your plate and bring it in?" You hate the way you sound and feel, but it's too late now. Two minutes later, that plate is still there and you've had all you can take. You pick up the plate and bring it into the kitchen before heading back to Grace. You grab her iPhone and say, "You can have this tomorrow." She looks surprised, "Jeez, what's the big deal? I was going to bring in the plate, but then you did it for me." You walk away exhausted and literally nothing has changed. You brought the plate in, she didn't seem to really understand the situation at hand, and you are more tired than if you'd just done it yourself without the yelling.

Humans just love to talk. It's inherent in our being. Even introverts talk more than animals do. We don't take enough time to listen and give time for the other person to see that we mean it and that we'll wait. The more clear we are about what we'd like our children to do, and the more often we expect the same thing, the more likely they are to understand the expectation and learn to do it.

There are a few very good reasons why kids don't do what we ask them to do after the first time they are asked:

- Kids don't share our priorities.

- We've trained kids not to do what we ask until we're hysterical.

- Kids need us to help them transition to the new task.

- The part of the brain called the frontal cortex, which makes decisions, is still developing.

- Kids don't feel heard.

- Kids are disconnected from adults.

THE MANTRA: LET MY DECISION STAND

Now that you have a lot of information about your child's current capabilities and have made decisions about what skills you want your child to learn, you are ready to think about how this plays out on a daily basis. This is a place where parenthood gets a bit sketchy. You have to teach these new skills, but you also have to continue to reinforce the skills you previously taught. It takes a lot of fore-thought and a lot of discipline, but don't let that scare you off. One of the great things about parenthood is that, like childhood, everyone learns as they go.

There will be some days when you say it once and your child gets up and does it right away. If this ever happens (and I do mean ever), please take the time to sit back and enjoy the experience. The more you feel good about it, the more likely you are to try to repeat this experience. In many ways parenthood is just a series of experiences (both good and bad) you get to store up for future use.

Let My Decision Stand is not as easy as it sounds. There are lots of other things that must come into play to ensure that you can say it once and mean it. The reason I say to do it as often as possible is that it will feel impossible at first. You'll need to choose things that are already pretty clear to your child. It's also important to remember that lots of kids take things literally. You'll need to learn how to say, "Pick all the Legos off the floor and put them in the containers where they belong," instead of, "Clean up the playroom."

You'll also need to learn how to remove the distractions and emotions that surround your child at the exact moment you want her to do something. Have you ever played basketball? Me neither, but I have seen it played. You know that part where one player has the ball and suddenly all these other players are all over that player trying to stop her from sending the ball into the air the way she wants it to go? That's what it feels like for a kid when we give them instructions to do something while they are doing something else. And, they're pretty much always doing something else. Do you see where I'm going here? It's tough to get their attention, and once you've said it once, you aren't supposed to say it again. So you'll need to get their undivided attention if you want to follow the mantra *Let My Decision Stand*.

> **Don't be wishy-washy about things. State what you need your child to do in as few words as possible and don't add extraneous information.**

WHAT YOU CAN DO TOMORROW

In the case of, "Say it once and mean it," start small. It's easier to maintain your sanity when you aren't dealing with something that matters a lot to you. Let's say you want your child to take a shower:

- **Observe your child in the moment.** You need to figure out what your child is doing and how engrossed she is right in this moment. It is here that you'll start to consider what this player needs in order to get the ball in the basket.

- **Remove the distraction by assisting with transition.** Approach your child and ask about what she is doing. "What game are you playing? How's it going? What do you need to do in order to feel done with this game or at a good place to leave it for a bit?"

- **Listen and wait.** This is where you need to employ your self-restraint skills because if you use this time to say what you want her to do right now, you are almost guaranteeing that you will have to say it again. She isn't ready to really hear you. Let her step out of her zone and be a bit more receptive to your request. It's not always going to work, but you need to give this part a try and make it your usual mode of operation. This is where so many kids have trouble these days. Electronics and other modern distractions are fantastic at keeping the brain totally engaged. The more your child learns how to break away when necessary, the better.

- **Say it once.** When you catch your child's eye and you feel the breaking point, say, "Okay! It's time for you to get in the shower ... right now." Then stand there staring at her until she heads in the right direction. If this happens relatively quickly, praise the heck out of her. You might even say, "It's awesome that you did what I asked so quickly. That means you'll have more time tonight to do (whatever it is she loves to do at night)." Show her that her ability to move past distraction and on to the productive activity is a lesson that will serve her well.

A BLUEPRINT FOR FULL IMPLEMENTATION

Step 1: Use the mantra.

This is not only a lesson in parenthood but a lesson in self-control. This is where a mantra is particularly handy. Another mantra like this is *H.A.L.T.,* where even the mantra itself reminds you to stop and think. So stop right now and say three times:

Let My Decision Stand
Let My Decision Stand
Let My Decision Stand

Step 2: Remove distractions; help plan for transition.

There are lots of ways to do this step, but right off the bat it requires you to stop and think about what your child must stop before transitioning to the thing you'd like her to do. Take a look at Template #8 to see how you might phrase your requests. Your priority is not necessarily her priority. There are several ways to help a child learn to transition. First, you need to break down the process so you can be sure it's clear. Does one activity need to be stopped and cleaned up before another can begin? Then ask her to do that first. Too many steps at once mean repetition down the road. Planning the steps helps you say it once and stick to it. Ease into transitions whenever possible. When a child is particularly invested in an activity, it will be harder for him to stop doing it and focus on what you want him to do.

Step 3: Focus on what you want to be done, not on why you are mad.

When children take a long time to get to the task we want them to do, it's irritating. There are so many things in play here that we begin to make parenting choices out loud as a threat. "You watch too much television. This is ridiculous! I'm not letting you do this ever again." These kinds of threats will absolutely slow the process down and shut your child's brain down. You are guaranteed to have to repeat yourself at this point because the focus on the new task has been redirected to panic about the removal of fun—forever. What you know is a temporary loss of sanity (on your part) is truth (on their part).

Step 4: Learn to clearly state your request.

Don't be wishy-washy about things. State what you need your child to do in as few words as possible and don't add extraneous information. "Please put all of your Lego bricks in the yellow container," is much more likely to be remembered by your child than, "Please clean up after you play with your friend. Don't always leave it such a mess. We're going to the park after, and I want to come home to a clean house." This opens the focus door wide and let's all kinds of distractions in.

Step 5: Ask your child to repeat what you said.

This does two things: It helps your child stop and focus on what needs to be done, and it ensures that you will not have that conversation. "Oh, you told me to make my bed? I didn't hear you say that." If there is repetition in the discussion, let it be your child's and not yours. You are going to say it once after removing distractions and you are going to ask for it to be said back to you to be sure it was heard.

Step 6: Wait.

Give your child time to move into the next activity. Your time is different from her time. If you grew up having to get right on something immediately, lest your parent flip out, this will take some practice. If there is a time crunch, add that into the equation when you make the request, but don't make a habit of waiting until the last second to ask your child to do something. Assume it will take longer. She is learning and practicing. It is not established yet. It's fine to stand there as gentle pressure. Teachers do this all the time. When a student isn't doing what she is supposed to be doing and the teacher is sure the student knows what to do, a good teacher will come in close proximity to that child. This proximity adds the mild pressure it sometimes takes for someone to do the right thing.

Step 7: Say thank you.

Show your gratefulness, even if your child is doing something that is supposed to be done. I read once that Marie Kondo, author of

The Life-Changing Magic of Tidying Up, believes you should thank your shirt (or whatever) for making your life better. If you can thank a shirt, you can thank your child. I like to think that the "thank you" is also to the universe for making your day easier. When your child begins to stop, look, and listen in order to follow directions, your parenthood universe will feel better. And that is worthy of saying "thank you."

OVERCOMING PUSHBACK

The pushback here will be either from yourself or from other people who are watching. The pressure of having other people judge you can be tremendous. The fact that everyone else is either a parent already or had a parent already means that everyone thinks they are an expert. You are learning techniques that will build a stronger parenthood. They can do things their way—but give yourself room and permission to do it your way.

I have to say it again or she won't know what to do. You are right. If you haven't followed the first steps for removing the distraction, you will need to repeat your decision. Try to stop and think before you ask your child to do something. Remember that you may not reduce the time it takes for your child to do the thing you asked him to do, but you aren't making yourself crazy by repeating what you want over and over. Not only does this repetition teach your child to respond when she feels like it or when you are hysterical, but it also teaches her to beg until you give in.

I can't stop and think every single time! Sure you can. It will be a new way to parent, for sure, but it is totally possible to plan before each time you ask your child to transition. If teachers can do it with twenty-four kids in the classroom together, so can you.

Children should respect their parents enough to do what is being asked. My guess is that older people will say this the most. The older generation is used to saying something and having it obeyed more instantly. They are also used to associating punishment with inaction. When punishment is your primary recourse, the relationship suffers, and a good relationship is the key to honesty. We're looking at the big picture here and hoping you can avoid shooting yourself in the foot by getting your child to do one thing at the expense of another.

THE MANTRA IN ACTION

For the most part, the *Let My Decision Stand* issues can be fixed with a schedule. When children know what to expect every day, they tend to follow along with the routine. That said, parents tell me regularly that they cannot get their child to turn off one activity and move to the next without an Act of Congress. Even mild-mannered teachers tell me that saying it once and meaning it requires a completely different mindset. We're going to use the mother of a child with Asperger's syndrome to show us how it's done.

Aileen Hower is a teacher and the mother of three children. Her oldest, Liam, is on the spectrum. She needs to make sure he learns to follow cues so that he can be successful in life and get out of it what he wants, and what she wants for him. Here is her story:

"With Liam, I always needed to get his attention. I could not just talk to the back of his head with the television on and expect him to 'hear' me. Rather, I would need to turn off the TV, ask him to look at my face, state the command or ask him a question, then get his response. I would sometimes need to sing his name to get him to focus on me. Once focused, he was ready to listen and comply.

In order for him to be the type of kid who, when I started to count down, would not wait until I got to 'one' to respond, I had to make sure he knew that counting was the last way I was going to get his attention. We have had success in sharing with Liam's teachers that he needs a warning before switching from a preferred to a non-preferred task. This has helped him be more flexible and change activities with less meltdowns.

At home, he would be playing a video game. We would ask him to pause the game, look at our faces, and share that there were only five minutes left before we had to shut off the game. It's important to know that if you stop some games before you finish a level, all of your work is lost. This was important to learn, as well as which games could be paused and which could not.

At one minute before we needed to transition to a new activity, I would ask Liam to pause the game again, look at my face, and say, 'One minute. What do I need to happen in one minute, Liam?' This time, he was the one who shared what would happen. This helped create ownership over the transition.

When time was up, we would announce, 'Time is up.' Then we would try to create excitement about what was to come next, especially if it was less preferred than what he was doing. 'Are you ready to …?' Or, 'Let's get ready to …' Or even, 'I can't wait to …' so that he didn't feel like he was leaving something great for something horrible.

This routine helped him learn about and manage his time. Eventually, we would announce five minutes (we've always had to give him the warning), and he would end after three or four minutes when the level was finished. He learned that he couldn't start a new level, so he didn't need all of the extra time."

Wow, right? If she can do that with Liam, I know I can be better at removing distractions so that I can *Let My Decision Stand* whenever possible. Can't you? It's a work in progress to be sure, but it's so worth it.

I learned about the mantra *Let My Decision Stand* when I was training dogs to guide blind people, and it has become one of my most valuable parenting skills with my children. It takes practice and consistency to say something once and mean it, but this expectation for automaticity will help your child remove a lot of procrastination from his life and get things accomplished. It has also improved our family relationships and reduced household stress all-around.

THE WORLD REALLY IS DIFFERENT

Curate What's Important and Block Out White Noise

Try something different. Surrender.
— RUMI

THE PROBLEM: THINKING WHAT WORKED FOR YOUR PARENTS WILL WORK FOR YOU

IN EVERY GENERATION there are people who will say, "Back in our day this never would have happened." I nearly waffled here telling you that this might be true occasionally, but I stopped. The truth is that the world is so completely different from what it was twenty-five years ago and earlier, that we can never think what we're dealing with during our parenthood is comparable. Sure, you'll be able to recreate experiences and some of those amazing childhood feelings you had, but they will be created in a vacuum. You will have to shut out the world in order to make them happen.

We now have constant access to a steady stream of information through TV, tablet, laptop, and phone. Even kids as young as five or six often have access to those devices. Don't worry though; I'm not going to tell you it's bad for them. I mean maybe it is, but Cool Whip was bad too, right? There are things that we need to take control of in our lives, and electronics is a pretty big undertaking. In fact, the ability to pick and choose what comes into your life and block out the rest is a skill we have to master in order to be a successful adult. It's a skill that many adults are struggling with every day.

It's easy to ignore the need to help your child master how to curate information during the day. "Curate" is a verb which means to select, organize, and look after items in a collection. When we pick and choose what we engage with on the internet and in our daily lives, we prioritize and compartmentalize them. This is tantamount to how the brain works. In building this skill, we are teaching our children to function as a brain. That is, to simultaneously take in bits of information and sort them quickly to ensure the least distraction; throwing out the stuff that doesn't need to be remembered.

Make devices work for your family, enriching your life and challenging you, instead of overwhelming you.

If you think this isn't critical, let me tell you about a couple of eighteen-year-old young men who didn't know how to do this when they got to college. They both arrived for their freshman year, thrilled to be there. They were ready. In high school, they had worked hard on their grades, played baseball and soccer, and already had some high school friends going to the same school. Their parents had planned for college enough so they shared the debt with their sons. Both young men failed their first semester. Both stated they were overwhelmed and didn't know how to get their work done. Both felt they didn't know how to shut out the constant stream of social media in order to get to their homework and personal needs. One sought therapy the college provided on campus but dropped out for a semester anyway. The other left college for good. Their moms are friends of mine who don't know each other. This is common; ask your friends whose kids go to college. It's tough to shut out the white noise of the digital world.

Helping our children learn to curate and moderate information is critical to becoming a successful adult. The first step in this process is to buy into the mantra that *The World Really Is Different*.

YOUR MANTRA: THE WORLD REALLY IS DIFFERENT

This may be a lesson you need to learn for yourself before you can teach it to your child. I am guilty of bringing my phone to bed despite my husband asking me not to. If I can't always shut out the incoming information, how is my child supposed to accomplish it? Information is fascinating and sparks our curiosity, but our brains also need time to process it. You aren't a colander that lets things flow quickly out; instead, you're more like a cheesecloth. By this I mean that you have the ability to filter out the big chunks of info you don't need, but you might need to push and prod the small unimportant things to go away and stop clogging your brain.

With this *The World Really Is Different* mantra, you will be teaching your child to set goals around gathering information on a device. He'll need to be able to discuss which part of his device time was spent mindlessly being entertained, and which part was gathering neat info for a wonder session or for a class. In this way, people can start to take control of their devices instead of letting marketing control them.

When we start to see how companies are using us for their benefit, we realize how important it is to take back the control. Just as I have to make healthy choices about food or plan how to get in and out of Target without spending a hundred dollars more than I intended, I also have to make choices about how I want to use my device. One day I realized that my phone called to me more than two to three times an hour! I really didn't need to know when every single Facebook friend liked or commented on something. So I turned off my phone notifications for all my social media apps. It took two weeks before I stopped picking it up to check each app. It's highly addictive to have people liking you and commenting on things you do all the time.

For our children, it's even more addictive because they've never lived without it. Especially when they are feeling insecure or uncertain, that social app can make them feel better. It can also make them feel much worse. Letting a device come into your home should be an invitation to make your life better, and the only way to ensure that concept is working is for each individual to take control of her devices and how she uses them.

WHAT **YOU** CAN DO TOMORROW

Start to have dinner table conversations about the role of devices and incoming information in your family life. Ask your child how he feels about your device use. Be brave—you might not like what you hear. Tell him how you feel about his device use. Make an agreement to have two hours per day free of devices.

- **Set a two-hour time frame during waking hours when no device will be present.** You might make mealtimes device-free. I suggest making homework time social media-free. The two hours might be broken up into half-hour increments. Do what works for you, but be sure that two hours of your life and your child's life are visibly device-free each day. You'll be surprised, I think, by how hard that is to do at first. The purpose of this is to show your child how to block out social media distractions and get some work done or find some time to process. We use 5-7 p.m. because that means we prepare dinner together, eat dinner, and spend some time as a family without a device distracting anyone.

- **Put your device in its spot.** Agree to ground rules, such as: Devices must be on the front hall table or in a basket in the kitchen. It doesn't matter where they are, but having a spot to put them marks the device-free time.

- **Talk about what information you learned or saw today.** If we never use the information we are looking at during the day, is there really a point to gathering it? This conversation helps kids see when they are productively using their

devices and when they are wasting time. Time will always be wasted on devices, but consciously discussing issues may start to reduce the waste and increase time spent for useful purposes. *The World Really Is Different,* and dinner table conversations must evolve to include topics about our digital lives, too.

A BLUEPRINT FOR FULL IMPLEMENTATION

Step 1: Have a family meeting to talk about device use.

This is an important step because unless we are intentional about our device use, we will always make snap decisions about it. It's important to avoid the constant giving and taking away of devices as punishment. I know most of you just rolled your eyes because you've come to know devices as the only currency you can use with your child. The problem with this is that it makes devices more illicit and inherently interesting. They become like junk food.

At this family meeting, talk about how great devices are for curating information as well as for entertainment. Use Template #9 to identify a few ways you can use your device productively. Then, you can each share one or two ways you gather information or get things done with your device. I encourage you to resist the urge to tell your child that what she does with her device is not as important as what you do. This happens, believe me; I know from experience. This is an open forum for talking about what devices and information mean to each of you. When this conversation is open, your child will feel free to tell you when a device is consuming her life.

Step 2: Set a daily time frame as device-free.

For most families, this will be just before, during, and after dinner. Two hours is enough time to start to remember that life goes on without a device, but if you need more, make your time longer. The purpose of device-free time is to set up a daily routine where you and your child can process information and focus on those around you. If you have younger children, this time may be much longer. If you have older children who aren't home very much, that two-hour time span can be tough to fit in. But once you make a conscious effort to get device-free time into your lives, you will start to notice the difference. Device-free time is for you to help your child value other priorities and reflect on digital use. Instead of mindlessly watching a show, your child will need to come up with a conversation about what he watched.

Step 3: Actively seek and share interesting sites with your child.

Don't assume your child knows how to find good information. When I was a teacher, I spent many hours curating good sites for my students to check out during their research projects, because the internet can be too vast to be helpful, and too grown-up for younger kids. Some teachers would tell me they relied on apps that were designed to vet sites and information, but I felt that it was valuable to have adult human eyes looking at the sites too. My son and I challenge each other to find cool sites with new information we didn't know before. I also ask my kids about what they are learning and try to find sites that complement those topics. The more you share with your child, the more you'll learn about him. Is he obsessed with only one topic? Does she stay on one site for just a few seconds before flitting to another? What types of online information does she find funny?

Step 4: Turn off app notifications.

Even when our devices aren't near us, they are calling our names. When you turn notifications off, you spend less time running to your phone or thinking about it. It's easy enough to turn everything off except for important regular alarms or calendar reminders. This is a lesson in learning how to control your device and not let it control you. This is also where older kids start to have issues. You know your child best, but when you see a device calling out to your child with a constant buzz and ding and a string of notification icons at the top, it may be time to change how the phone is working for him.

Step 5: Use your device as a learning tool at least once a day.

Instead of passively using your device, consider using it as a learning tool at least once a day. For kids learning a new language, change the phone language to the language they're learning. This helps them see how other kids their age would see the same phone and helps them learn in an authentic way. Help your child add apps like Kahn Academy to his or her phone. This app used to be just about math but has expanded into housing cool video-driven courses, like one from Pixar about storytelling.

For your outdoorsy kids, have them add an identification app for plants or birds. They can spend hours finding the answers to questions to which you used to say, "I don't know, let's find out." For your writers, there are notetaking apps and ones with timed daily writing exercises. For artists, there are drawing apps and videos to show them how to create what they want, step-by-step. I've used Art Hub for Kids very successfully with those who feel they can't draw anything or who want practice. There are apps being created every day that teach us things or direct our passions instead of passively letting them control us. *The World Really Is Different*, but this isn't a bad thing. In fact, it's pretty awesome.

OVERCOMING PUSHBACK

Digital consumption and control is a new landscape, and people will want to tell you how to navigate it. Everyone fancies himself an expert in how screen time is destroying our lives, so you'll need to be ready for the pushback.

Devices are terrible. I can't believe you let your kids use them so much. Devices are no longer optional. There will be people who tell you they don't have them or use them, but they are few and far between. Devices are useful, brilliant, and very entertaining. It's how we control our devices that makes all the difference. You can tell these naysayers that you are teaching your child to control his device so it doesn't control him. End. Of. Story.

We only allow screen time from 4-5 p.m. You are so permissive. Even my pediatrician says it's bad. There is no way to avoid screens unless you don't go to school and don't have a TV and don't have a phone and don't have a job. The trick is in making decisions about passive screen-watching, but that's the same trick as making decisions about eating junk food. You are just reflecting on your passive device use compared to your active and engaged device use. It is this controlled use of screen time that will make the difference between accepting that *The World Really Is Different*, or pretending that we still live in an age without smartphones.

Isn't your device-free time just like my screen time in terms of rules? Well, no. Device-free time is to recharge your human interaction skills and engage in discussions that help you process the information you've just learned on your devices. We can value the tools without giving ourselves over to them. There is nothing wrong with using a tractor when your lawn is so big. There is so much information out there and we want to learn to rein it in to make it work for us, not against us. So instead of "tune-out time" solely as a break from devices, we use this time to process and discuss our online activities. *The World Really Is Different.* The differences have their benefits worth talking about around the dinner table.

THE MANTRA IN ACTION

A common theme in our culture is that electronic devices are inherently bad for people in general and kids in particular. Parents are regularly told to reduce screen time. This can cause a lot of fighting in a household. I've often wondered about fight reduction as a form of parenting. "What can I do to ensure we don't fight about this?" The best answer I can come up with is that the more you talk things through and the less you post edicts that are inflexible, the more likely you are to keep the peace.

My end goal for my children is that they will be able to control their electronic devices and make them work positively for them. They also need to use their devices to improve their lives and help them learn. Sometimes this is the joy of exclaiming, "I'm looking that up! I don't believe you." Sometimes that means saying, "I read this on the internet, what do you think about it?" Most of all it means not using a device mindlessly in order to bide your time in life. Instead of blaming screens and devices for the disconnection between you and your child, figure out what you could be teaching and modeling in order to change your child's habits.

At our house, device use is pretty much a free-for-all. Did you gasp? Are you putting this book down because you think I'm a crackpot? First of all, I do it my way; you do it your way. No judgment. This works for me. I want my kids to learn from the start that they have to put the device down when it's getting in the way of their accomplishments. I also don't have a secret app that tells me every stroke they make. I do require that I have the passcode to their devices in case I need to check something, but for the most part I don't snoop around. Instead we have a device-free time when we talk about what they watched, and what they think about a new app or video that came out. My kids are just ten and twelve at this writing. Things may have to change a bit when they get older, but I hope not. I want them to go to college doing the right thing for themselves even if I'm not there watching.

I am a strong believer in helping kids develop intrinsic motivation to take good care of themselves. I don't know how kids are making it through college without this skill. We can't always be doing whatever we want until or unless someone catches us. That's not a healthy way to live.

When my friend Sarah's three kids come home, they head to the kitchen to deposit their phones in a device basket. It's second nature to them now, but it was tough to enforce at the beginning. Until their kids, Catherine (seventeen), Daniel (sixteen), and Benjamin (twelve) got into middle school, they hadn't developed a plan for devices. One night as Sarah and her husband Chris were sitting at the dinner table, they realized that no one was talking to each other anymore. They felt like dinner should be a natural check-in place where they could see what their busy teenagers and pre-teens were thinking, doing, and feeling. The devices they held stopped them from sharing who they were right now.

So Chris and Sarah sat down one night and created a plan to develop a device-free time in their house. They found a basket that could easily hold all five devices and they decided to choose the time right after school until after dinner as device-free time. It was less of a time limit and more of a feeling. This would give their three kids time to do homework and slow down after their day at school. This would give parents time to focus on their kids. "It was amazing how fast we started learning about what they were up to and how they were doing," Chris said. That simple new device habit was developed out of need, and it changed the way devices were perceived. Catherine now says she plans to have a device-free time when she heads to college. Mission accomplished.

When it comes to devices, you have to be clear and consistent. There is too much constant information flowing through, and all of us could benefit from having a regular goal to step away from our devices and process what we are learning and doing online. Accepting that *The World Really Is Different* means making intentional changes to accommodate our new world and retain our parenting ideals. Realize that there are no common parenting rules around digital use. We are going to have to develop it as we go based on what works best for our families. The information coming in is powerful and fascinating, but it must be processed and controlled. Fight first to control the devices around you and then help your child do the same. Make devices work for your family, enriching your life and challenging you, instead of overwhelming you. Curate what's important and block out the rest.

MANTRA 10

INSTINCT TRUMPS RULES

Trust Yourself Even When Everyone Tells You Not To

*When you do things from your soul, you
feel a river moving in you, a joy.*
— Rumi

THE PROBLEM: YOU HAVEN'T DONE THIS BEFORE SO IT'S HARD TO TRUST YOURSELF

In short, parenthood is the biggest lesson in humility and self-exploration you'll ever have. What makes it doubly hard is that just when you think you have it down with one kid, the next requires something totally different. You have to learn to go with your gut.

Okay, I know what you're thinking. "Wait a minute. Are you saying that I should ignore everything you just explained and solely rely on my instincts?" Let me put your mind at ease. I'm not saying that at all. What I am saying is that understanding human behavior and making educated assumptions about the "why" is more important than tracking the number of times someone does something on her own.

> **Every time you learn to avoid the danger of doing something that doesn't work for you and your child, you build your instinctual muscles.**

Most important, don't let your ego get in the way of making the right decision. It can be easy to fall into the trap of thinking that your children represent you. When they are acting up in front of other people, you want to push back and get it under control fast, but consider how your insides feel. Might it be better to back away from your child and wait it out? Using the *H.A.L.T.* mantra is good for more than just identifying your child's needs; it's also good for taking stock of how you feel about what's happening.

Why is trusting your instincts so powerful? Because your brain has been cataloging a whole lot of information for as long as you've been alive. It functions even when you aren't conscious of it. Sure, we've been working on intentional parenting, but we would be missing an enormous component if we didn't spend a chapter on intuition. Just as your child knew to look for food within hours of being alive, so do you know what's best for your child. Parenting books come in handy to help us sort through all the external stuff that humans have created—but the heart of parenting is truly just you and your child.

YOUR MANTRA: INSTINCT TRUMPS RULES

When my son was about seven months old, everyone kept telling me it was bad for us to be sleeping in the same bed. Though it was easy for us and we got loads of sleep, I thought other people must be right. There was no problem to be solved, but other people made me feel like I needed a solution. Isn't that crazy?

I read about putting a baby in his crib and letting him cry it out. I gently placed him in his crib, gave him a kiss, sang him some songs, and walked out of the room shutting the door behind me. He cried the second the door clicked shut. Then he proceeded to cry for more than two hours. I sat on the stairs sobbing. My stomach felt sick. Those people who told me to do this weren't anywhere. You know that feeling? That uncomfortable feeling when the situation just isn't sitting right with you? I felt confused and torn.

Almost no one enjoys being confused because it doesn't feel safe. Confusion typically triggers a mild, or sometimes severe fight or flight response. And by the time you get to that point, you are either ready to attack, retreat, or simply freeze. You have a built-in mechanism called "instinct" that is there to help guide you through life, but sometimes you don't listen to it. Sometimes you listen to another part of you—maybe that's your compassion or your fears. And often the path you should take is the one you avoid. In that moment alone on the stairs, I realized that I had started where I wanted to end. I was fine with us jumping into bed together early at the end of a long, baby-filled day. I was more than fine with it; I enjoyed it. Being close together at night felt cozy and completely fine until someone told me it wasn't good parenting.

I stood up, went into the room where my baby was hiccupping because he was so hysterical, and picked him up. I brought him back into my room where he fell asleep almost before his head hit the pillow. Then I promised him that I would do better at listening to my instincts and myself, and I apologized for my misstep that evening. It would be one among many missteps in his childhood

117

that have generally turned out to be valuable lessons about following my instinct.

Instinct is a survival mechanism attributed to evolution and it contributes to the survival of our species. It becomes strengthened and smarter over time because of our experiences. Every time you learn to avoid the danger of doing something that doesn't work for you and your child, you build your instinctual muscles. You strengthen and smarten the mechanism that makes your parenthood unique to you and your child. You can get pretty darn good at it too.

The philosopher Aristotle shared this wisdom: "We are what we repeatedly do. Excellence, therefore, is not an act, but a habit." Essentially, he is saying that we can change who we are by mimicking the way we want to become. This is the philosophical forerunner of "Fake it until you make it."

Start small. Pick an area where you tend to second-guess yourself. Stick with your original answer. Act on the basis of that answer and see what happens. If you are a parent who breaks promises, keep one small one. Even if it is minuscule, it is still a promise kept. The more promises you keep, the more you develop a habit of keeping promises. At some point, you may reach a place of recognizing that you are reliable and that you (and others) may see you as a parent who keeps her promises. As you begin to work on how you perceive yourself, you must also begin to internalize the mantra, *Instinct Trumps Rules*. When you trust yourself and your parenting, you will know how to make decisions for this child, who is, after all, the love of your life.

WHAT **YOU** CAN DO TOMORROW

If trusting your instincts is new to you, take some steps to start doing it more often, starting tomorrow!

- **Pay attention to your body's reactions.** Use your PRN to help you make sense of what you feel. Check out Template #10 to see an example and try this out for yourself. Write about the people who make you feel confident and the ones who make you feel bad. Noticing your emotions and body reactions is the first step to reconnect with your gut.

- **As you go through your day, notice the signals your gut tries to send you.** Maybe you're wondering whether or not to stop your child from Facetiming a friend while doing homework. Don't calculate the answer. Stop controlling it, and ask your body, "Should I leave her alone, or tell her to end the conversation?" Relax into the new sensation of letting your body (not your brain) make decisions for you.

- **Stop and attend when your body signals you.** Let no twinge go unaddressed. If you are by yourself, name the twinge out loud. "Uh-oh, I was just thinking about how much TV Jack is watching, and my stomach lurched. I need to pay attention to that." Pause and reflect on the message your intuition sent you. You will never go wrong listening to yourself.

> • **Change the path if it doesn't feel right.** If you get this queasy feeling about Jack watching too much TV, go in and tell him you will be turning it off in five minutes. Tell him you want to play a game or bake brownies with him. Change the path until the queasiness goes away. Trust your body to know when to change course. When *Instinct Trumps Rules,* you won't feel like it's a failure to make mistakes and change course.

A BLUEPRINT FOR FULL IMPLEMENTATION

Step 1: Pay attention to how you feel about your parenting.

I hope this book inspires you to start paying attention to how you feel about your parenting. If you are always feeling less than other parents, then you may want to start a regular mantra practice. You have the tools needed to make a difference in your parenthood. Take the time to pay attention. If it's hard for you to do that, download an app like Headspace to help guide you. You have to parent 24/7, so you should also consider how you did every day. This doesn't have to be a long and involved process, just ten minutes a day of checking in with yourself can be considered a meditation practice.

Step 2: Spend time with people who reinforce you.

There will always be people who criticize how you parent and who you are. You must work to stay away from them. If you are comfortable with the way you parent and how your children are functioning in the world, then there is no reason to let someone else interfere.

This doesn't mean you should surround yourself with people who don't offer you anything. Some advice is great, some is necessary, and support cannot be underestimated. You might think it's fine to cater to your children, but perhaps you are showing signs of exhaustion. A good friend will be brave enough to tell you to let the kids do some things for themselves so that you can sit once in awhile and relax.

I have a habit of wanting everyone in my household to have pleasant mornings. I avoid morning conflict like the plague. One day a friend was watching me get up no less than twelve times to get everyone at the breakfast table the thing they wanted in the moment they wanted it, though they were all capable of getting it themselves. She laughed and said to my son, "Hey, the fridge is just as close to you as it is to her, get it yourself." At first I felt miffed, like, "Don't tell my kid what to do," but then I realized she was right. I deserved to sit at the table and eat breakfast too. My friend's supportive input was invaluable.

Step 3: Daydream about your children.

What would you like to see happen in their lives? Don't censor the ideas that come to you. The more you tell your body, "Go ahead and steer me where I need to go," the louder its guidance will become. Just as with our own selves, it is easy to see how people can think smaller instead of grander. Dream about your child's future as a famous presenter, surgeon, or engineer. Find positive traits in her that you know she could build on and share those with her. Let her know that you see her skill in the kitchen and that she might end up being a chef like Gordon Ramsay (except maybe less rude). Find shows for her to watch like MasterChef Junior that help her see how to channel her abilities and find passions. When we don't allow ourselves to think big, we become too narrow in our plans for ourselves and our children.

Step 4: Before heading to sleep, review your day's responses to your child.

The best way to learn from your behavior is to check in with yourself at the end of the day. Think about your positive reactions and fear reactions. Review times you were proud of your parenting and times when you could have done better. Re-enact the events in your mind and ask, "What was my body trying to tell me?"

When my children get hurt, I have been known to yell at them. It sounds crazy, but I believe that my fear converts to anger over why they would let their precious bodies be unsafe. I love them so much, and it panics me to think of them in pain. I have to check in with myself quickly when someone is hurt to remind myself that they are probably okay. Our children need us to make rational decisions and have calmer reactions to life's daily situations. Let yourself replay the situations but this time, improve your responses. How might it have played out? Try that next time. Be aware that the social stories we tell ourselves about who we are as parents can be adjusted and retold in ways where you star as the loving, kind, and joyous parent you know you can be.

Step 5: Be aware of the tapes in your head that will tell you to listen to someone else.

Don't leave your body out of the decision-making process and only listen to your busy brain. Practice telling the voice in your head to step aside because you want to get your body's guidance, too. It is hard to retrain our brains to trust ourselves, but it is possible. If you've been someone who always listens to other people because you feel like you always mess up with your kids, start small. Use your PRN to write out small moments when you followed the mantra, *Instinct Trumps Rules* and experienced great parenting. That dinner everyone loved where the family chatted and laughed, without a phone in sight? Write it down. That bath time when you didn't rush it and you let your son play with the measuring cups as long as he wanted? Write it down. Gather up those great experiences so that when times are tougher, you'll remember that you know how to do things well. This way you can always get back to feeling good about your parenting just by opening up your PRN.

OVERCOMING PUSHBACK

This is one of those places where there will be a lot of pushback. Not only will people tell you what to do, but they will also make you feel that you aren't right for parenting or that your child will turn out badly. Don't panic. You can trust yourself. It's such a touchy subject that people who become parents must fight back vigilantly by trusting themselves and their instincts, even when it seems easier to give in to others. Remembering the mantra *Instinct Trumps Rules* regularly will help keep you in the moment.

Why are you letting her talk back to you? That's disrespectful. If you know that you are giving your child voice and choice over her life and what happens to her, you might look like a parent being disrespected once in a while. If this comes up when someone else is watching and makes a comment about it, calmly tell the person that your child has every right to let you know how she feels. You may want to let them know that you plan to give her guidance and discuss the issue at hand after she has shared. When you know why you are parenting the way you do, you can feel more comfortable letting other people know that their way isn't your way.

You're leaving the party because of your child? Don't let him control your fun. If you see that your child is tired and you follow *H.A.L.T.,* you know that it's in everyone's best interest if you head home to let your child sleep. Instead of arguing with someone at a party, just laugh and say, "I love that you are going to miss us! Thank you for that." Then you'll laugh and shrug and think about how much easier it will be to get your little one to sleep so you can sit back and have a glass of wine in peace.

Everyone else is doing the project for their kid. This may be true, but your child will learn better by doing it himself, plus you want him to have the experience. He worked so hard to choose the materials for the project. He knows he can ask for your help when needed. It may be hard for you (or your child) to see professional-looking products returned to school when his looks like a five-year-old made it, but then again, he may be so super proud of his own that the difference won't matter. Your instinct is telling you it's better to take a step back as a parent. *Instinct Trumps Rules,* and while it doesn't always make the choice feel great, it usually ends up making the choice feel right.

THE MANTRA IN ACTION

I asked parents to chime in and let me know when they let *Instinct Trump Rules,* because it comes up over and over. You'll need all ten mantras regularly to help you stick to this one! Here are a handful of the responses from parents:

"I ignored a lot of advice about sleep. I thought my daughter needed to be rocked, so I rocked her. I thought she needed to nurse, so I nursed her. Now she is five and she asks me to pat her back, so I pat it." — Emily, mother of one

"I let my older son quit baseball mid-season, breaking our own rule about living up to commitments. The team situation and sport itself were a bad fit for my Jake. He wasn't learning new skills or enjoying any part of it. He dreaded practice and games to the point where it seemed cruel to make him finish out the season. I spoke with the coach, also a friend, who thought it would be harder on Jake to quit and be embarrassed by that decision, but I had a gut feeling we needed to leave the team and move on from baseball ASAP. I think it was the right thing to do. Jake has been careful about signing up for commitments since then and doesn't think we're always going to bail him out. — Susan, mother of two

"My younger son kept complaining that he didn't want to wear shoes at school because they felt "too spicy." The teacher was irritated because he kept taking them off and thought he was being difficult. He had time-outs as a result. I thought there must be something other than behavioral problems involved and looked at his feet and shoes for the answer. It turned out his shoes, made by a Japanese company, used green tea in the soles of the shoes to keep them smelling fresh. They were spicy! The herbal quality of the tea was irritating his feet." — Susan, mother of two

"I let my daughter stay up much later than any of her friends when she was in middle school. She had a lot of trouble sleeping and she didn't seem to be tired during the day. Our rule with our other kids was no electronics or lights after 10 p.m., but this kid ran differently. After constant yelling and fighting, we determined that this kid had a different body clock. We stuck to no electronics, but let her read and draw late into the night." — Cathi, mother of three

"Two of my triplets weren't sleeping at all at six months. The experts all said to let them cry for hours upon weeks on end. I felt something wasn't right and stopped after the second night of "sleep training" and started thinking of health reasons. Turned out they had a corn allergy (which their doctors didn't believe until I demanded a test, by the way) and as soon as I eliminated it they slept pretty well." — Jody, mother of triplets

"The first night after my second was born, he slept through the night. The nurse admonished me for not waking him for a feeding. I just nodded and assured her I would the next night. LOL, as if! I declared him the best baby in the world and never woke him to feed. No weight issues, just an awesome sleeper! I wondered just how I would wake myself but never bothered to ask." — Sine, mother of two

Trusting your parenting intuition takes courage because nearly every week you'll encounter a new situation that requires you to make a decision, but it is not impossible. Trusting and believing in yourself is more important than trusting others. You have to start by considering your past success at parenting. Nothing is too small to consider. Somewhere along the way things went exactly as you hoped and planned that they would. Call on those good feelings. Look back and think about what led up to your success and try to replicate those steps. Just as you can get used to failing, you can get used to succeeding. Focus in on your past victories and use them to build trust in your abilities moving forward.

Even though self-trust needs to come from within, it can be a big boost to hear reinforcement from someone else. It doesn't need to be an impartial person, either. Talk to a close friend or family member. Ask them to reinforce why they believe in your parenting intuition and why you should believe in it yourself. Many of our doubts come from fear that others will judge us. A big step toward total trust in yourself can come from letting go of concerns about what others are thinking. You will never control the thoughts and actions of other people—and spending time and energy worrying about them is a waste. An attitude adjustment like this takes time, but it will be worth it in the end. Using mantras is an excellent place to start to look inside and find your confidence. They cut out the noise of daily life and allow you to focus on yourself and your parenting. Above all else, *Instinct Trumps Rules*.

CONCLUSION

PARENT MANTRAS

Life is a balance of holding on and letting go.
— RUMI

I MAY NOT HAVE cracked the code on parenting, but I think all parents would agree that the best course of action as a parent is to trust yourself. It's easier said than done, and the ten mantras you've learned in this book can help you stay the course. It's so easy to fall off the path, no matter how beaten the trail. If you remind yourself to reflect and move forward every day, you'll be giving your kids exactly what they need: a reflective, honest, loving parent.

Becoming a parent was, for me, a dream come true. I promised to do the best I could and make sure my kids felt loved and secure.

When I fail to do that, I notice they still learn from me. Perfection doesn't teach them anything. They do learn from the times I say I'm sorry and from watching me make intentional and transparent changes about how I parent them and how I live my life. When I chose to leave teaching to become a full-time writer, my kids were proud of me. You could see it every time I told someone about my new job. Being a parent has helped me become fearless about living the best life I can every day. The people who love me best are watching and I want them to see that being their parent is a gift to me. Sometimes that gift is hidden under arguing and tough days, but it's always easy to find when I need it most.

For most of their childhood, kids are in school. This made a book like *Hacking Parenthood* a perfect member of the *Hack Learning Series*. I hope you'll use all the resources available to you to help these children who you love so much. Whether books are geared toward parents or teachers, parents can read them to gain so much valuable information about raising and teaching children. I use every resource I can find to keep me informed about best practices and to stay open to learning more about how to raise my children. If you want to share what you've learned, I'd love to hear about it. I can be reached on Twitter @kimberleygmoran or on our Facebook group Hacking Parenthood.

PARENT

RESOURCE

NOTEBOOK

MANTRA 1
SEEK TO UNDERSTAND

EXAMPLE

Child's current age: <u>6 years old</u>

What are milestones for a 5-7 year old? Conduct a Google search for "developmental milestones 0-19 years old."

Kids in this age range have a high energy level. They attempt all kinds of physical feats. They have the physical skills for game playing. They like to build and create things. They can pay attention and shift attention. They are able to give more thought to decisions. They are very interested in collecting things. They begin to see others' points of view. They show an interest in books and music. They have fewer questions but the questions are more meaningful. They want to be treated like an adult. They can accept fair punishment. They feel hurt when called names. They are proud and possessive of belongings. They worry about being liked. They enjoy talking more than cuddling with parents.

Recent milestones	Milestone goals
Dresses himself	Makes bed
Sets the table	Keeps own room clean
Understands what rules are	Keeps backpack organized

TEMPLATE #1

Child's current age: _____

What are milestones for your child's age range?

Recent milestones   **Milestone goals**

-   -

-   -

-   -

-   -

MANTRA 2
BEGIN AT THE END

EXAMPLE

Child's current age: 6 years old

What are traits you'd like your child to have?

Think for oneself

Read to entertain or inform

Follow through on a passion

Find motivation for an activity

Have a conversation

Feel compassion for others

Listen appropriately

Clean a room

Organize things

Trait	Goals to reach trait
Clean a room	Makes bed, folds and puts away clothes, has a place for toys and belongings
Have a conversation	Talks about 1-2 things that happened during day. Identifies something another family member might want to talk about

TEMPLATE #2

Child's current age: _____

What are traits you'd like your child to have?

Trait   **Goals to reach trait**

-                                    -

-                                    -

-                                    -

-                                    -

MANTRA 3
CHOOSE TO UNICYCLE

EXAMPLE

Child's current age: <u>6 years old</u>

Unicycle Chart

Skills	Tallies
1. Makes bed	||
2. Finds belongings	||||

TEMPLATE #3

Child's current age: _____

Unicycle Chart

Skills	Tallies
1.	
2.	
3.	
4.	

MANTRA 4
ANSWER THE QUESTION ASKED

EXAMPLE

Child's current age: 8 years old

Important topic: DEATH

Answer

All living things die, but I've got lots of time to spend with you.

TEMPLATE #4

Child's current age: _____

Important topic: _____

Answer

Important topic: _____

Answer

Important topic: _____

Answer

MANTRA 5
HUNGRY. ANGRY. LONELY. TIRED. (H.A.L.T.)

EXAMPLE

Child's current age: 4 years old

Possible ways to solve these important needs

Hungry

— Bring healthy snacks with you wherever you go.

Angry

— Say, "I see this is something that's making you angry. What can I do to help?"

Lonely

— Offer to play a simple game for 5 undivided minutes of attention.

Tired

— Pull out a picture book and read to your child so he can begin to relax.

TEMPLATE #5

Child's current age: _____

Possible ways to solve these important needs

Hungry

—

—

Angry

—

—

Lonely

—

—

Tired

—

—

MANTRA 6
THE PRIZE IS IN THE PROCESS

EXAMPLE

Child's current age: <u>11 years old</u>

Challenge: Do the dishes

Process

1. Prepare the dishes: Make sure you have them by the sink and they are scraped free of food.

2. Prepare the water and soap: Make sure the water is warm enough and you have dish soap.

3. Rinse dishes and fill the dishwasher first: Make sure you rinse off items and stick them in the dishwasher. Put the plates in the bottom, the cups on top, and the silver in the basket.

4. Wash pots, pans, and cooking dishes: Dip them in soapy water and use a scrub brush or sponge to get the food off. Put them in the dish rack to dry.

5. Wipe down the sink and your tools.

6. Put away your supplies and you're done.

When a child is doing these steps, regardless of outcome, make sure to praise a step accomplished well.

TEMPLATE #6

Child's current age: _____

Challenge: _____

Process

1.

2.

3.

4.

5.

6.

MANTRA 7
HONESTY COMES WITH TRUST

EXAMPLE

Child's current age: <u>13 years old</u>

Characteristics people have

— Smile

— Sense of humor

— Hair

— Clothing style

— Hobby

— Passion

How to show similarities

"When you smile like that, you remind me so much of myself."

"I know you like sweatshirts like I do, so I got you one too."

TEMPLATE #7

Child's current age: _____

Characteristics people have

—

—

—

—

—

—

—

—

How to show similarities

MANTRA 8
LET MY DECISION STAND

Say it once and mean it. Kids take things literally, so ask for exactly what you want to have happen.

EXAMPLE

Child's current age: 9 years old

What you want	What you'll say
A clean playroom	"Pick all the Legos off the floor and put them in the containers where they belong."
Food and plates back in the kitchen	"Please move the two glasses, bag of chips, and crumbs to the kitchen sink and trash."

TEMPLATE #8

Child's current age: _____

What you want   **What you'll say**

MANTRA 9
THE WORLD REALLY IS DIFFERENT

EXAMPLE

Child's current age: <u>16 years old</u>

Device: iPhone

Ways to use device productively

Using a GPS to plan a trip

Checking a weather app to see how to dress for the day

Leaving a message on Voxer for a study group

Reading a book on the Kindle app

Listening to a podcast that helps you learn more about a topic

TEMPLATE #9

Child's current age: _____

Device: _____

Ways to use the device productively

—

—

—

—

—

—

—

—

—

—

MANTRA 10
INSTINCT TRUMPS RULES

EXAMPLE
What happened? Who was involved?

My son was born and my mother thought breastfeeding wasn't necessary. Every time I pumped, she acted like I was wasting my time. I finally decided breastfeeding was too difficult and gave my son formula which was okay for him but not what I wanted.

How did you feel?

I felt unsure of myself and like no one was respecting my wishes. I didn't feel supported. I wish I'd found someone who could have helped me breastfeed instead of relying on someone who didn't think it mattered.

People who build you up

Make a list of people who are a good support system for you.

- NICU nurse
- Friend who breastfed her three children

TEMPLATE #10

What happened? Who was involved?

How did you feel?

People who build you up

Make a list of people who are a good support system for you.

—

—

—

—

—

OTHER BOOKS IN THE HACK LEARNING SERIES

HACKING EDUCATION
10 Quick Fixes For Every School

By Mark Barnes (@markbarnes19) & Jennifer Gonzalez (@cultofpedagogy)

In the bestselling *Hacking Education*, Mark Barnes and Jennifer Gonzalez employ decades of teaching experience and hundreds of discussions with education thought leaders to show you how to find and hone the quick fixes that every school and classroom need. Using a hacker's mentality, they provide **one Aha moment after another** with 10 Quick Fixes For Every School—solutions to everyday problems and teaching methods that any teacher or administrator can implement immediately.

"Barnes and Gonzalez don't just solve problems; they turn teachers into hackers—a transformation that is right on time."

— DON WETTRICK, AUTHOR OF PURE GENIUS

MAKE WRITING
5 Teaching Strategies That Turn Writer's Workshop Into a Maker Space

By Angela Stockman (@angelastockman)

Everyone's favorite education blogger and writing coach, Angela Stockman, turns teaching strategies and practices upside down in the bestselling, *Make Writing*. She spills you out of your chair, shreds your lined paper, and launches you and your writer's workshop into the maker space! Stockman provides five right-now writing strategies that reinvent instruction and **inspire both young and adult writers** to express ideas with tools that have rarely, if ever, been considered. *Make Writing* is a fast-paced journey inside Stockman's Western New York Young Writer's Studio, alongside the students there who learn how to write and how to make, employing Stockman's unique teaching methods.

"Offering suggestions for using new materials in old ways, thoughtful questions, and specific tips for tinkering and finding new audiences, this refreshing book is inspiring and practical in equal measure."

— AMY LUDWIG VANDERWATER, AUTHOR AND TEACHER

HACKING ASSESSMENT
10 Ways to Go Gradeless in a Traditional Grades School

By Starr Sackstein (@mssackstein)

In the bestselling *Hacking Assessment,* award-winning teacher and world-renowned formative assessment expert Starr Sackstein unravels one of education's oldest mysteries: How to assess learning without grades—even in a school that uses numbers, letters, GPAs, and report cards. While many educators can only muse about the possibility of a world without grades, teachers like Sackstein are **reimagining education**. In this unique, eagerly-anticipated book, Sackstein shows you exactly how to create a remarkable no-grades classroom like hers, a vibrant place where students grow, share, thrive, and become independent learners who never ask, "What's this worth?"

"The beauty of the book is that it is not an empty argument against grades—but rather filled with valuable alternatives that are practical and will help to refocus the classroom on what matters most."

— *Adam Bellow, White House Presidential Innovation Fellow*

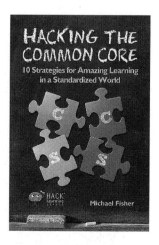

HACKING THE COMMON CORE
10 Strategies for Amazing Learning in a Standardized World

By Michael Fisher (@fisher1000)

In *Hacking the Common Core,* longtime teacher and CCSS specialist Mike Fisher shows you how to bring fun back to learning, with 10 amazing hacks for teaching all Core subjects, while engaging students and making learning fun. Fisher's experience and insights help teachers and parents better understand close reading, balancing fiction and nonfiction, using projects with the Core, and much more. *Hacking the Common Core* provides **read-tonight-implement-tomorrow strategies** for teaching the standards in fun and engaging ways, improving teaching and learning for students, parents, and educators.

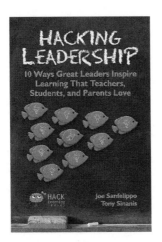

HACKING LEADERSHIP
10 Ways Great Leaders Inspire Learning That Teachers, Students, and Parents Love

By Joe Sanfelippo (@joesanfelippoFC) and Tony Sinanis (@tonysinanis)

In the runaway bestseller *Hacking Leadership*, renowned school leaders Joe Sanfelippo and Tony Sinanis bring readers inside schools that few stakeholders have ever seen—places where students not only come first but have a unique voice in teaching and learning. Sanfelippo and Sinanis ignore the bureaucracy that stifles many leaders, focusing instead on building a culture of **engagement, transparency, and most important, fun.** *Hacking Leadership* has superintendents, principals, and teacher leaders around the world employing strategies they never before believed possible.

"The authors do a beautiful job of helping leaders focus inward, instead of outward. This is an essential read for leaders who are, or want to lead, learner-centered schools."

— GEORGE COUROS, AUTHOR OF THE INNOVATOR'S MINDSET

HACKING LITERACY
5 Ways To Turn Any Classroom Into a Culture Of Readers

By Gerard Dawson (@gerarddawson3)

In *Hacking Literacy*, classroom teacher, author, and reading consultant Gerard Dawson reveals 5 simple ways any educator or parent can turn even the most reluctant reader into a thriving, enthusiastic lover of books. Dawson cuts through outdated pedagogy and standardization, turning reading theory into practice, sharing **valuable reading strategies**, and providing what *Hack Learning Series* readers have come to expect—actionable, do-it-tomorrow strategies that can be built into long-term solutions.

HACKING ENGAGEMENT
50 Tips & Tools to Engage Teachers and Learners Daily

By James Alan Sturtevant (@jamessturtevant)

Some students hate your class. Others are just bored. Many are too nice, or too afraid, to say anything about it. Don't let it bother you; it happens to the best of us. But now, it's **time to engage!** In *Hacking Engagement*, the seventh book in the *Hack Learning Series*, veteran high school teacher, author, and popular podcaster James Sturtevant provides 50—that's right five-oh—tips and tools that will engage even the most reluctant learners daily.

HACKING HOMEWORK
10 Strategies That Inspire Learning Outside the Classroom

By Starr Sackstein (@mssackstein) and Connie Hamilton (@conniehamilton)

Learning outside the classroom is being reimagined, and student engagement is better than ever. World-renowned author/educator Starr Sackstein has changed how teachers around the world look at traditional grades. Now she's teaming with veteran educator, curriculum director, and national presenter Connie Hamilton to bring you **10 powerful strategies** for teachers and parents that promise to inspire independent learning at home, without punishments or low grades.

"Starr Sackstein and Connie Hamilton have assembled a book full of great answers to the question, 'How can we make homework engaging and meaningful?'"

— DOUG FISHER AND NANCY FREY, AUTHORS AND PRESENTERS

HACKING PROJECT BASED LEARNING
10 Easy Steps to PBL and Inquiry in the Classroom

By Ross Cooper (@rosscoops31) and Erin Murphy (@murphysmusings5)

As questions and mysteries around PBL and inquiry continue to swirl, experienced classroom teachers and school administrators Ross Cooper and Erin Murphy have written a book that will empower those intimidated by PBL to cry, "I can do this!" while at the same time providing added value for those who are already familiar with the process. *Hacking Project Based Learning* demystifies what PBL is all about with **10 hacks that construct a simple path** that educators and students can easily follow to achieve success.

"*Hacking Project Based Learning* is a classroom essential. Its ten simple 'hacks' will guide you through the process of setting up a learning environment in which students will thrive from start to finish."

— DANIEL H. PINK, NEW YORK TIMES BESTSELLING AUTHOR OF DRIVE

HACK LEARNING ANTHOLOGY
Innovative Solutions for Teachers and Leaders

Edited by Mark Barnes (@markbarnes19)

Anthology brings you the most innovative education hacks from the first nine books in the *Hack Learning Series*. Written by twelve award-winning classroom teachers, principals, superintendents, college instructors, and international presenters, *Anthology* is every educator's new problem-solving handbook. It is both a preview of nine other books and a **full-fledged, feature-length blueprint** for solving your biggest school and classroom problems.

HACKING GOOGLE FOR EDUCATION
99 Ways to Leverage Google Tools in Classrooms, Schools, and Districts

By Brad Currie (@bradmcurrie), Billy Krakower (@wkrakower), and Scott Rocco (@ScottRRocco)

If you could do more with Google than search, what would it be? Would you use Google Hangouts to connect students to cultures around the world? Would you finally achieve a paperless workflow with Classroom? Would you inform and engage stakeholders district-wide through Blogger? Now, you can say "yes" to all of these, because Currie, Krakower, and Rocco remove the limits in Hacking Google for Education, giving you **99 Hacks in 33 chapters**, covering Google in a unique way that benefits all stakeholders.

"Connected educators have long sought a comprehensive resource for implementing blended learning with G Suite. *Hacking Google for Education* superbly delivers with a plethora of classroom-ready solutions and linked exemplars."

— DR. ROBERT R. ZYWICKI, SUPERINTENDENT OF WEEHAWKEN
TOWNSHIP SCHOOL DISTRICT

HACKING ENGAGEMENT AGAIN
50 Teacher Tools That Will Make Students Love Your Class

By James Alan Sturtevant (@jamessturtevant)

50 Student Engagement Hacks just weren't enough. 33-year veteran classroom teacher, James Alan Sturtevant, wowed teachers with the original *Hacking Engagement*, which contained 50 tips and tools to engage teachers and learners daily. Those educators and students got better, but they craved more. So, longtime educator and wildly popular student engager Sturtevant is *Hacking Engagement Again*!

"This book is packed with ideas that can be implemented right away: Some creatively weave technology into instruction, others are just plain creative, and all of them are smart. Plus, the QR codes take the reader to so many more fantastic resources. With this book in hand, every teacher will find ways to freshen up their teaching and make it fun again!"

— JENNIFER GONZALEZ, BESTSELLING AUTHOR, SPEAKER, AND CEO AT CULTOFPEDAGOGY.COM

HACKING DIGITAL LEARNING STRATEGIES
10 Ways to Launch EdTech Missions in Your Classroom

By Shelly Sanchez Terrell (@ShellTerrell)

In *Hacking Digital Learning Strategies*, international EdTech presenter and NAPW Woman of the Year Shelly Sanchez Terrell demonstrates the power of EdTech Missions—lessons and projects that inspire learners to use web tools and social media to innovate, research, collaborate, problem-solve, campaign, crowdfund, crowdsource, and publish. The 10 Missions in *Hacking DLS* are more than enough to transform how teachers integrate technology, but there's also much more here. Included in the book is a **38-page Mission Toolkit**, complete with reproducible mission cards, badges, polls, and other handouts that you can copy and distribute to students immediately.

"The secret to Shelly's success as an education collaborator on a global scale is that she shares information most revered by all educators, information that is original, relevant, vetted, and proven, combining technology with proven education methodology in the classroom. This book provides relevance to a 21st-century educator."

— Thomas Whitby, Author, Podcaster, Blogger, Consultant,
Co-founder of #Edchat

HACKING CLASSROOM MANAGEMENT
10 Ideas To Help You Become the Type of Teacher They Make Movies About

By Mike Roberts (@BaldRoberts)

We've all seen the movies. A teacher faces a lackluster educational environment or encounters a classroom full of downtrodden students. Not only do movie teachers solve those problems, they make a profound impact in the process. Many educators set out to be that kind of teacher, and then reality gets in the way. The success or failure of a class hinges on effective classroom management. Modeling concepts through both real-world scenarios and via some of the best educators in cinema, Mike Roberts, the 2014 Utah English Teacher of the Year, proves that learning to manage a classroom like a movie teacher is easier than you think. The best part is you can nail the role with just a few simple tweaks to what you're already doing. The book's **10 classroom management hacks** will guide you there. To make things even easier, Roberts gives readers a peek "Behind the Scenes" of successful classroom management with a bonus activity, prompt, or template in each hack.

HACK LEARNING RESOURCES

All Things Hack Learning:

hacklearning.org

The Entire *Hack Learning Series* on Amazon:

hacklearningbooks.com

The Hack Learning Podcast, hosted by Mark Barnes:

hacklearningpodcast.com

Hack Learning on Twitter:

@HackMyLearning

#HackLearning

#HackingLeadership

#HackingLiteracy

#HackingEngagement

#HackingHomework

#HackingPBL

#MakeWriting

#HackGoogleEdu

#EdTechMissions

#ParentMantras

#MovieTeacher

Hack Learning on Facebook:

facebook.com/hacklearningseries

facebook.com/groups/hackingparenthood

Hack Learning on Instagram:

hackmylearning

The Hack Learning Academy:

hacklearningacademy.com

MEET THE AUTHOR

 Kimberley Moran is first and foremost the mother of Felix (twelve) and Annie (ten). When she was just eleven years old, she set up a daycare center in the small shed next to her summer house. Three or four young kids came each day to be read to, taken to the library, and taught songs. She has always wanted to raise children. So, she became a teacher first and later a mother. She also loves to write and is currently an editor at WeAreTeachers.com where she gets to write about teachers, children, and their families. You can find her on Twitter @kimberleygmoran. Please join in the conversation about parenting using the hashtag #parentmantras.

ACKNOWLEDGEMENTS

IF I'M HONEST, I'm grateful for the hundreds of experiences and forces that make me the kind of person who just does stuff. I never think something is out of my reach and for this, I am profoundly thankful because it has brought me so many gifts.

To my husband, Dick Moran, who is my biggest fan, who thinks I can do no wrong out in the world, who wouldn't be surprised if I told him I was going to run for president (I'm not). It is this kind of support that makes someone feel strength and courage when the going gets tough. I love you so.

To my children, Felix and Annie Moran, who make my parenthood the most exceptional experience of them all. I am eternally grateful for the fact that you are mine and you are amazing. The world is just as lucky to have you in it, as I am. I love you too.

To the many parents out there in the world who shared their life's work with me through tears and laughter. We put a lot at stake when we become parents, but more so when we take this miraculous task seriously. I wish all of you Parent Resource Notebooks filled with the scrawls of your hopes and dreams for your beautiful children.

To Mark Barnes who believed in me enough to ask me to write the book he had been hoping to see. Your perseverance and support helped me know this was possible.

To Rebecca Morris, who is beyond brilliant. You took my thoughts and words and ideas and made them say what I wanted to say. It takes care and intelligence and purpose. You've got all three. Thank you.

To the children who have been mine when I was a teacher, you are still mine. Being a teacher made me a better parent and being a parent made me a better teacher. Without you, I wouldn't have that. When I see one of you in the grocery store and your eyes light up or you poke your parent to say that Mrs. Moran is in aisle six, it makes me feel like even more of a parent.

And finally, to my own mother and father, Anne Spencer and Guy Gorelik, despite every troubling thing out there in the universe, you loved me and I knew it.

Times 10 is helping all education stakeholders improve every aspect of teaching and learning. We are committed to solving big problems with simple ideas. We bring you content from experts, shared through multiple channels, including books, podcasts, and an array of social networks. Our mantra is simple: Read it today; fix it tomorrow. Stay in touch with us at HackLearning.org, at #HackLearning on Twitter, and on the Hack Learning Facebook group.

Made in the USA
Columbia, SC
09 September 2020